knits
to fit & flatter

knits

to fit & flatter

DESIGNS TO MAKE
YOU LOOK & FEEL FABULOUS

**JANE
ELLISON**

David and Charles
www.mycraftivity.com

A DAVID & CHARLES BOOK
Copyright © David & Charles Limited 2009

David & Charles is an F+W Media Inc. company
4700 East Galbraith Road
Cincinnati, OH 45236

First published in the UK in 2009
First published in the US in 2009
Reprinted 2010

Text copyright © Jane Ellison 2009

A catalogue record for this book is available from the
British Library.

ISBN-13: 978-0-7153-3146-0 Paperback
ISBN-10: 0-7153-3146-9 Paperback

Printed in China by RR Donnelley
for David & Charles
Brunel House, Newton Abbot, Devon

Commissioning Editor: Jennifer Fox-Proverbs
Editorial Manager: Emily Pitcher
Editor: Verity Muir
Project Editor: Nicola Hodgson
Art Editor: Sarah Clark
Production Controller: Ros Napper

David & Charles publish high quality books on a wide
range of subjects.
For more great book ideas visit: www.rubooks.co.uk

Contents

Introduction

I have always loved knitting. I love the rhythm of it and how soothing it can be. At the end of each day I have to knit a little (though usually I knit a lot!). Revelling in the creativity and the excitement that such simple stitches can create amazing knitted textures is how I relax after a busy day. In this book I take this inspiring activity and show you how you can use knitted fabrics to create beautiful, stylish garments that truly fit and flatter your body.

Although I love knitting, I have not always loved knitting patterns. When I was younger I would try to follow knitting patterns, but invariably became frustrated as they seemed so complicated. Because of this experience I want all of the knitting patterns that I design to be simple and straightforward to follow. To me, a knitting pattern is something that you can change to make into your ideal garment. At first this may seem daunting, but in this book I hope to gently guide you through and demonstrate how easy it is to make one of my patterns perfect for you, adjusting it if necessary so that it fits and flatters you. My designs are intended to be easy to adapt so that body lengths and sleeve lengths, for example, can be changed to fit you exactly; after all, there is no other person who has the same shape as you – you are truly unique, and the garments you create should reflect that.

> *"I hope my patterns inspire you to be creative and celebrate your beautiful, unique shape."*

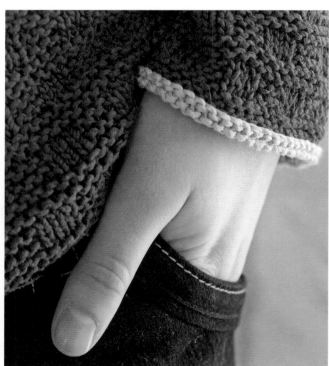

Getting started

This book will ensure that you make a garment that fits and flatters your body. I take you through measuring your body shape, measuring tension and how to change a pattern to suit your unique style. I look at different types of yarn, and importantly, how to substitute a yarn. I discuss the effects of different types of stitches to create knitted fabrics that will fit to your shape. I also consider different design details such as necklines, sleeves, the length of a garment, and the types of fastenings used. All of these elements can be used or adapted to create a garment that looks fabulous on you and fits you exactly how you want it to.

"Bring a fresh new approach to your body and your knitting. You are the perfect shape and knitting is the best way to create your own fitted, flattering garments!"

The projects

There are twelve projects in this book. We start off with sleeveless tops and summery garments. We then move through shrugs and lighter-weight sweaters and then on to the heavier-weight sweaters that will keep you looking stylish through autumn and winter, ending up with an elegant and versatile hip-length coat.

I want you to feel inspired by the designs and encouraged to make your own unique versions of the patterns. For that reason, I've included ideas for variations on the projects so you can see how versatile they are and the many ways they could be changed and adapted. Six of the projects have a 'Look again…' feature in which the design has been made up in an alternative colourway, maybe changing the yarn used, changing a trim, or altering a design element such as changing the length and shape of the sleeve.

Technique round-up

If you are reading a book on knitting garments, you are probably quite a confident knitter already. However, my designs are quite straightforward, and I would like relatively inexperienced knitters to feel that they could tackle these projects too. Just in case you need to brush up your garment-knitting skills, or are tackling this topic for the first time, I have included a section on techniques at the end of the book (pages 113–126). Here I outline the techniques that you will need to make the garments, including making buttonholes, picking up stitches (which you will need to do for some of the necklines), knitting with beads, and joining pieces together for a professional-looking finish.

Difficulty ratings

Each of the patterns in this book has been given a difficulty rating. Do not think that these are set in stone! What one knitter finds difficult may be very different for another knitter. Even if a project is labelled as 'Advanced', do not be put off making it if it really appeals to you. My designs, even the ones that are marked as being advanced, are still meant to be straightforward and approachable.

The ratings are:

 1 Straightforward

2 Intermediate

3 Advanced

Knitting tips

Where you see this symbol in the pattern instructions, I have included some practical advice that may help you with the making of the garment.

Fit and flatter tips

Where you see this symbol in the pattern instructions, I have offered some insight into how parts of the pattern have been written to fit and flatter you, and how you might adapt it to make it really suit you.

Measuring up

There are a number of things you need to know before you a knit a garment that successfully fits and flatters your unique body shape. It is very important to achieve the correct gauge. You also need to make an honest and accurate measurement of what size you are and what size garment you should make to achieve the best fit.

The importance of gauge

The first essential task to do before you start knitting your garment is to make a gauge square and check that your gauge is the same as that called for in the pattern instructions. This is a step that many knitters miss out. They then tell me that the resulting garment is too big or doesn't fit properly and ask me where they went wrong. If I ask them whether they made a gauge square, I might hear a variety of elaborate stories and excuses as to why they didn't. It's as if they know they should have and that this would be the solution to the problem, but they just haven't admitted it to themselves!

You may think that knitting a gauge square is a laborious task, but it is vital to the end result. Even being one stitch out in the gauge square can make the difference between two sizes. Consider this extract from a knitting pattern:

gauge
24sts and 40 rows to 4in (10cm) square over st st using size 3 (3.25mm) needles

measurements

to fit chest	extra small	small	medium	large	extra large
	32–34	36–38	40–42	42–44	46–48in
	81.5–86.5	91.5–96.5	101.5–106.5	106.5–112	117–122cm
actual	38¼	42¼	44¼	46¼	50¼in
measurement	97.5	107.5	112.5	117.5	127.5cm
length	21¼	21½	22	22¾	23½in
(excluding straps)	54	55	56	58	60cm

Cast on 117[129:135:141:153]sts

If your gauge means that you knit 25sts per 4in (10cm) instead of 24sts (that is, if your gauge is too tight), you might think it's only one stitch out, so it doesn't matter. Consider this, though: if you want to knit the medium size, 135sts divided by 24sts is just over 22in (56cm). However, if you divide by 25sts and the measurement changes to 21¼in (54cm), this means your knitted garment will end up being the small size. In this case, one stitch difference means one whole size difference in the end.

If your gauge is too loose, and you achieve 23sts to 4in (10cm), this will make the measurement of the finished garment 23 (58.5cm) – a whole size bigger.

Making a gauge square

A gauge square is measured over a 4in (10cm) square (although you make it slightly bigger than this size). Gauge is expressed as the number of stitches and rows in this square. In the example shown above, there are 24sts and 40 rows to 4in (10cm) square.

1 To make a gauge square, first cast on the number of stitches stated in the gauge part of the pattern, and then cast on an extra 4 stitches. Work in the pattern (in this example, stockinette stitch), until the square measures 4¾in (12cm).

2 Don't cast off; instead break the yarn and thread it through the stitches, taking them off the needle.

3 To count the stitches in your gauge square, lay it down flat. With stockinette stitch, a stitch makes a 'V' shape. Place a pin by the side of one 'V'. Then measure 4in (10cm) horizontally with a tape measure and mark this with a second pin. Count the number of stitches between the pins.

4 To count the number of rows, use your first marker to measure from again. Measure 4in (10cm) vertically down, and place a second pin. Count the number of rows between the pins.

5 If you have the stated number of stitches and rows between the pins then you have achieved the correct gauge and can commence your chosen pattern.

6 If you have too many stitches, your gauge is tight and your garment will be smaller than stated. Change to a larger needle and knit another gauge square. If there are too few stitches, your gauge is loose and your garment will be bigger than stated. Change to a smaller needle and repeat the process.

Tension – too tight

Tension – just right

Tension – too loose

Choosing the perfect size

Getting the tension right is the first step to knitting the right size garment. The second step is knowing and loving your individual size. Some knitters immediately choose by the label 'small', 'medium' or 'large', as this is the size they buy in the shops. This is not advisable; sizes can vary considerably from store to store.

It is very important to look at the 'Actual measurements' section of the knitting instructions. The 'To fit' sizes are suggested, whereas the 'Actual measurements' are, as they say, the actual size.

Once you have found a garment that you wish to knit, find a similar garment in your wardrobe that fits you or the person you are knitting for. Lay your existing garment out flat and measure across the chest (about 1in (2cm) under the armholes). Once you have this figure, compare it to the width measurements given in the pattern instructions and on the schematics (the diagram of the garment) and choose the knitted garment size that is nearest to this figure.

Adapting a garment

If you want to lengthen or shorten the garment, you need to do this before you reach the 'Shape armholes' instruction.

Measure the top of the shoulder by the neck to your desired length. Compare this length with the one in the pattern. If you want the pattern, for example, 4in (10cm) shorter, you need to take off 4in (10cm) from the measurement in the pattern before the 'Shape armholes' instruction.

For example, if the pattern says...

> Starting with a knit row, cont in st st until the back measures 12in (30cm) from the cast-on edge, ending with a wrong side row.

...change this measurement to 7¾in (20cm).

Don't forget to do this on the front too!

The same principle applies to the sleeves. Once you have knitted the back and front, pin or sew the shoulders together. Pin the side seams and put the garment shell on. Ask a friend to measure from the seam under the arm to your desired sleeve length.

To lengthen or shorten the sleeve, find the instruction in the pattern that states:

> Cont in patt without shaping until the sleeve measures 17¾in (45cm) from the cast-on edge, ending with a wrong side row.

...change this measurement by your different amount.

Designs to flatter

Cosy cables *is knitted in a gloriously chunky yarn. This style of garment will give the illusion of curves to flatter-chested, slender women.*

The most wonderful things about the female body are that it is curvaceous and that there is only one shape that is just like yours. For example, my sister and I look as though we have the same body shapes. We are the same height and the same weight. However, she has a longer torso and shorter legs while I have longer legs and a shorter torso. Therefore, if we knitted the same size pattern, the finished garments would look different from each other.

> " *It is very difficult to see yourself as you truly are and love the shape you are, but once you do it is extremely liberating!* "

The garments I designed for this book are intended to flatter and enhance your natural beauty and perhaps give you the look of a curve where there might not really be one. The most important thing to remember is to not cover up! Many people think that the best thing to do with their clothes is to use them like tents and that covering up their body makes them look better. This is not true! It just makes you look shapeless and hides all the beauty that you have.

Opposite I give an outline of which garments might best flatter you, according to your shape. I then focus on individual design elements, such as necklines, sleeves and fastenings, that can be used to create a flattering look.

Creating a nipped-in waist

The *Lace-edged wrapover* (pages 56–63) is perfect for those of you who don't have a defined waist. The V-neck, the cropped length, and the tie around the waist all help give the illusion of a slender waist. The *Shawl-collar cardigan* (pages 64–71) is fastened with a single button under the bust. This is good for creating a flared shape from the waist to the hips, again giving an illusion of a shapely waist. The *Ruffled up vest top* (pages 28–35) in mohair yarn with edging detail is also ideal for creating the illusion of a waist; the yarn carefully follows the body under the bust while the ruffle edge sits away from the body and therefore gives a beautiful curvaceous shape.

Flattering a large bust

A V-neck or scooped neck is a great detail for those of you with large breasts. The low neckline helps to breaks up the expanse of the chest. The *Silver shimmer shrug* (pages 50–55) is a good example of this; the V-neck will flatter your cleavage, while drawing the eye down to the waist, where this garment is tied.

Balancing out a pear shape

For those of you who are the classic pear shape, you don't always have to cover your hips. Choose the *Push the boat out sweater* (pages 72–77), as this neckline helps balance out the hips. Alternatively, if you wear the *Great lengths coat* (pages 104–111) fastened at the waist it will gently skim over the hips, highlighting your neat, trim top.

The Silver shimmer shrug *is a great choice if you want to de-emphasize a larger bust; the V-neck gives you shape while breaking up the expanse of the chest.*

The Huggable hoodie *is a versatile everyday garment. The stretchy stitch pattern is figure-hugging and flattering to all sorts of body shapes*

The Two-yarn tunic *features an empire waistline and has a gentle A-line shape; two great design elements if you want to disguise your belly.*

The Great lengths coat *is a stylish choice if you are a little pear-shaped; you can wear it buttoned to the waist and it will then flare out flatteringly over your hips.*

Flattering a small bust

Those of you who are a little more flat-chested can flatter your figure with the *Cosy cables* poloneck jumper (pages 92–97). This heavy sweater with an intricate allover cable pattern will create the appearance of a fuller bust.

Disguising a belly

The stomach is central to us, both physically and emotionally, yet it seems to get a lot of bad press. The belly celebrates everything that is great about a woman, but sometimes this greatness doesn't need to be shown to everyone!

If you want to disguise your belly, the *Twice as nice cardigan* (pages 84–91) is a good option; it has a ribbed stitch over the chest, which means it will fit closely over the bust, but then falls more loosely in stockinette stitch, which falls delicately down to the hips.

The *Two-yarn tunic* (pages 42–49) is another winner here, as the focus is at the chest. This design features an empire waistline just under the bust, so the rest of the garment skims over the stomach and hips.

The *On the button tank top* (pages 36–41) has detail at the top and the hips with the underrated garter stitch in between. The garter stitch creates fabulous texture that hangs delicately from and over the bust, gathering at the hips, helping to hide that belly prettily!

The *Kimono-sleeved smock* (pages 78–83) is inspired by the empire line, as is the Two-yarn tunic, but in this instance I have used a cable stitch pattern to create detail at the bust. The rest of the garment then flows into stockinette stitch, which helps to cover the belly in a flattering way.

Lengthening the neck

Many of the garments here are perfect if you wish to create the illusion of a longer neck. The *Lace-edged wrapover, On the button tank top, Two-yarn tunic* and *Shawl-collar cardigan* all help to do this, as the depth of the neckline and detail away from the neck creates a beautiful space and therefore an illusion of a long and elegant neck (as long as you do not wear a crewneck or poloneck top underneath).

Showing off the bum

So many women want to cover up their bums! Again, this is something that makes women curvaceous, and should be celebrated. The *Shawl-collar cardigan*, if worn with a flared skirt, helps celebrate the curves that the waist and bum create, as the cardigan is nipped in at the waist to enhance the hips. The *Two-yarn tunic, Kimono-sleeved smock* and *Great lengths coat* all gently fall just below the bum, so they hide the area but tease the eye!

Something for everyone

My *Huggable hoodie* (pages 98–103) was designed with comfort in mind but with style right next door. Everyone has an old faithful that they throw on most days, and some of these garments can look shapeless. I designed this hoodie to be the everyday garment that looks great on everyone and is comfortable to wear without being shapeless. The cabling hugs the body shape, while the button detailing can be fastened up to the neck for those with a small chest or left undone for those with a larger chest to create detail and define the bust.

The Kimono-sleeved smock is a longer garment, flowing gracefully over the bottom and hips.

Necklines

My favourite neckline is the scoop neck, as featured on the *Twice as nice cardigan* (pages 84–91) and the *Kimono-sleeved smock* (pages 78–83). It is very flattering to all shapes and sizes; on busty women it helps to breaks up a large expanse of chest, while those with smaller chests can wear a scoop neck over a T-shirt or shirt. The soft, rounded shape also frames the face and neck nicely.

A boatneck such as that on the *Push the boat out sweater* (pages 72–77) is flattering on smaller-busted women. The horizontal, raised neckline makes it look as if you have a larger expanse of chest than you really do. A collar, such as that on the *Shawl-collar cardigan* (pages 64–71), is also a good choice for flatter-chested women, as the eye is drawn to the detail of the collar. A poloneck such as the one on *Cosy cables* (pages 92–97) is also great for women with smaller busts. The cables running down the front create a detail and texture as they lead the eye up to the poloneck, creating the perfect jumper for you. The long sleeves and longer length on the body and the neck make this jumper look very elegant on a small-busted woman.

V-neck or wrapover necklines, as featured on the *Silver shimmer shrug* (pages 50–55) and the *Lace-edged wrapover* (pages 56–63), are flattering for many shapes. They show off a larger bust and enhance curves whether they are there or not. V-necks also give the effect of a longer neck, which looks elegant.

The square neck detail of the *On the button tank top* (pages 36–41) is flattering for women with a larger bust; the neckline sits delicately above the bust and then drapes over the bust to gather at the hip, hiding all the bits we want hidden! The square neckline on the *Two-yarn tunic* (pages 42–49) is also flattering, but this time enhances the bust area and then flows into a lovely A-line shape that falls below the hip.

Sleeves

If you are worried about the size of your arms, then a good option is to go for an elbow-length or three-quarter-length sleeve. Both these lengths look chic, and also draw attention to your forearms and wrists, which are the narrowest parts of your arm. This creates a slimming effect. Several of my designs feature this length of sleeve, including the *Lace-edged wrapover* (pages 56–63) and the *Silver shimmer shrug* (pages 50–55).

I also like a bell-shaped sleeve, such as that on the *Kimono-sleeved smock* (pages 78–83). This creates a glamorous and flamboyant look, but also because the sleeve is so wide it makes the rest of you look slender by comparison.

I usually design sleeves that are easy to lengthen or shorten so you can adapt the pattern to make the sleeve the perfect length for you.

Garment lengths

My designs are very easy to lengthen or shorten. We all come in different heights and even people who are the same height overall may have different torso lengths. This is why it is important to measure yourself; you might be surprised at the actual length you need to knit.

For those of you who are pear-shaped, look for a design with a boatneck and then make sure that the length of the garment comes just to your hips, but does not cover them. This will help to balance out a pear shape.

If you want a design that flatters your stomach, look for a length that goes to your mid-thigh or knee with a button so that your waist is highlighted.

The length of a garment can affect its shape. If the garment is a jumper then it is a good idea to let it finish at your hips, while a jacket with button fastenings, such as the *Great lengths coat* (pages 104–111) can be longer and finish anywhere between your hips and knees. This is because the buttons can be fastened at the waist and therefore help create a flattering shape.

As always, it is a good idea to find a garment in your wardrobe that fits you well, then take the length measurement from this and apply it to the pattern.

A bell-shaped sleeve looks glamorous and dramatic, and draws attention to slender wrists.

A V-neckline is a flattering option for all sorts of body types, helping to emphasize a shapely figure and adding curves to a slender frame.

A scoop neckline makes a lovely frame for the face and elongates the neck.

A square neckline is a good feature for slimming down a broad torso; it also makes a great frame for a high-impact necklace.

It's easy to adjust the length of the Great lengths coat *so it is just right for you and flatters your proportions*.

Fastenings

I like to use fastenings to create individual details that are very simple to add but can help to transform a garment.

For example, the *Push the boat out sweater* (pages 72-77) has button details on the shoulder. This makes the eye go to the shoulder, one of the best parts of the body! A garment can be made truly individual depending on the buttons used. There are many lovely buttons available, including handmade ones that look like little jewels.

Fastenings are also great for creating shape. For example, if you fasten a button at the waist it creates a shape that enhances the natural curves – an effect seen on the *Shawl-collar cardigan* (pages 64-71). The one-button fastening at the waist creates a gentle shaping that looks lovely and curvaceous.

Tying a ribbon fastening under the bust is a great way to flatter the belly. The eye is drawn to the narrowest part of the torso and the bust, while the rest of the garment drapes down over the waist and to the hips. This is an effect that I've used on the *Two-yarn tunic* (pages 42-49).

The single-button fastening on the Shawl-collar cardigan *helps to create a shapely silhouette.*

The Push the boat out sweater *features a pretty detail of little buttons that fasten on the shoulders.*

Yarns to flatter

Yarns are addictive! Because I am a designer I have hundreds of hanks, balls, skeins and cones of yarn from many different yarn manufacturers; it all starts to build up! I still visit local yarn stores and get excited about seeing a different colour or a different fibre combination.

Which fibres are best?

Natural fibres, such as alpaca, silk, merino wool, mohair and bamboo are the best to knit with. These yarns, whether used alone or in blends, create luxurious yarns that are a joy to knit with. Each yarn can have a different feel and look. There are some yarns that drape more than others; for example, silk drapes heavily – a lot more than a mohair yarn, which is more like a fluffy cloud. Mohair isn't something that stretches as much as merino wool, which is a forgiving fibre with a lot of elasticity.

I design with the yarn first. I do some swatches with a yarn to understand how the fibres work and how they stretch, drape and feel. This can dramatically change the shape and look of a garment so it is very important to me, as a knitter and designer, to work with the yarn first.

For example, the beautifully soft 100% merino wool that I used for the *Huggable hoodie* (pages 98–103) is the right yarn for this garment. Wool is very forgiving; it stretches and then falls back into place without any strain on the fibre. The merino wool is also so soft that it feels like a lovely hug around your body.

The 100% silk used for the *Push the boat out sweater* (pages 72–77) has a luxurious feel and a drape that skims the body. The yarn feels gorgeous next to the skin.

A good example of how different yarns work and how that in turn can transform the shape and look of a garment is the *Ruffled up vest top*. In the mohair version (pages 28–33), it gently falls around the body, holding its shape while looking as if it delicately touches the skin. When knitted in 100% cotton (pages 34–35), the shape of the garment is changed; the cotton is heavier and although it does stretch slightly it doesn't delicately touch the skin, it holds onto it.

The chunky yarns used for the two versions of the *Great lengths coat* (pages 104–111) also produce a different effect because of their differing fibre content. Both yarns are mostly wool, blended with a smaller percentage of a luxurious fibre. The variegated version (pages 104–109) is knitted in a yarn that is 75% wool and 25% silk, while the solid-colour version (pages 110–111) is made in a yarn that blends 90% wool with 10% cashmere. Even with this relatively small change in the fibre blend, the difference is dramatic. The silk gives the wool a crisp feel and, because silk takes dye well, creates strong, rich colours. On the other hand, the cashmere is extremely soft and adds a cosy, smooth element to the wool fibre.

Bamboo is another beautiful yarn, which I used for the *Shawl-collar cardigan* (pages 64–71) in a blend of 80% bamboo to 20% merino wool. This creates a knitted fabric that has a wonderful sheen and softness, and is very fluid, so drapes flatteringly over your curves.

The ribbon used for the *Silver shimmer shrug* (pages 50–55) is an exception to my usual rule, as it is a synthetic fibre. Usually I go for yarns because of their stunning fibre content, understanding what each individual fibre brings to the blend. However, I was a little superficial with this design! I wanted a yarn that looked sparkly and glamorous. There are many ribbon yarns out there, but this one had the qualities of being fun to knit with and holding its shape better than alternatives (ribbon yarns can be a bit floppy when used for a garment).

"You can tell by touch when the best quality yarn has been used."

Substituting yarns

An exciting thing about knitting is that you can completely alter a pattern by knitting it up in a different yarn. This is something that you can experiment with, but it is also something to keep in mind when substituting yarn. You might want to use an alternative yarn (for example, if there's a yarn in your stash that you want to use, or if it's difficult to obtain the yarn specified) than that called for in the pattern, but still achieve the same sort of end result.

Always look for a yarn that has the same tension as that given in the pattern. This means that the garment will be the same size as given in the measurements, even if the look of the knitted fabric is different.

Take for example the *Lace-edged wrapover* (pages 56–63). The yarn used for the main project (pages 56–61) is 100% baby llama in a solid colour; the yarn used for the variation (pages 62–63) is a variegated yarn that is 45% silk, 45% mohair and 10% lambswool. The original top was knitted in the baby llama, and the smallest size took 9 balls. To work out how much yarn would be needed to make the variation garment, I looked at the meterage of the llama yarn (82yd/75m) and multiplied it by the number of balls used (9). So, 9 × 82yd (75m) = 738yd (675m). I then checked the meterage of the other yarn, which was 110yd (100m). I divided the 738yd (675m) by 110yd (100m), and worked out we needed just under 7 balls of the second yarn to make the variation garment.

This simple calculation is needed every time yarns are substituted.

These images show how different a garment can look when made in different yarns. You can see from these two versions of the Lace-edged wrapover that the llama yarn (the green version) has a heavier drape than the silk/mohair/lambswool mix (the rainbow stripe version).

Stitches to flatter

Stitch patterns are a great part of knitting. Often, all you need to create some amazing textures are just two stitches: knit and purl. How you use these can completely transform the garment. I love the fact that stitches can be used to create shape, which means that you don't have to work out where your hips or your bust are in relation to your waist. You can just change the stitch pattern while knitting the garment to create a bespoke fitted item.

" I find it irresistible to play with knit and purl stitches; with just these two key stitches you can get many variations and incredible textures. "

Designing with stitch patterns

When designing stitches, the yarn is the first thing I consider. For example, I played with the mohair yarn when designing the *Ruffled up vest top* (pages 28–35). This is a delicate yarn that I thought needed a lace pattern to show it off, and that also needed a ruffled edge to show off the fluffiness of the yarn. When I considered using a different yarn in the same tension I realized the ruffled edge lost its fluffiness.

One feature of my patterns is that I often use stitch patterns for shaping, rather than including increases and decreases. For example, the *Twice as nice cardigan* (pages 84–91) features ribbing over the bust and then falls into garter stitch rib. Ribbing is stretchy, so it holds its shape well over the curve of the bust. I then use garter stitch ribbing to fall delicately over the stomach and hips in a flattering flare.

The *Kimono-sleeved smock* (pages 78–83) is another example where there is no decreasing or increasing in the garment; all the shaping is done through changing the stitch pattern. The cable pattern at the top of the garment has a tighter tension than the stockinette stitch section. This means the garment will fit quite closely to the top of the body to flatter the bust, and then drapes over the stomach down to the hips to create a flattering shape.

Ribbing is my favourite way to create shape. Sometimes I add a little detail in with the ribbing, as in the *Shawl-collar cardigan* (pages 64–71), where the mock cable alternates with ribbing. This creates vertical lines running down the garment, which helps extend the torso and makes a slimming and flattering shape.

I think that garter stitch is often neglected. It is usually the first stitch you learn and as such it is dismissed as the easy stitch for beginners. I feel it can offer much more! It is a flattering choice for garments because it is stretchy and accommodating. The *Lace-edged wrapover* (pages 56–63) is made in garter stitch, and stretches easily around the body to flatter a wide variety of figures. Also because of the nature of the fabric you don't have to pick up stitches at the neck edge to create a neat finish; the garter stitch automatically makes a neat edge as you knit. The other fantastic thing about garter stitch is that it is reversible, so if you decide to knit the wrapover top without the ties and let it hang open, it will still look good.

Garter stitch is also great when used as a detail; for example, in the *Two-yarn tunic* (pages 42–49) the garter-stitch ridge creates the look of an empire waistline, which is flattering to the bust and is forgiving to those who don't have a defined waist.

I used garter stitch in another way for the *On the button tank top* (pages 36–41). The lace panel at the bottom edge has a tighter tension than the garter stitch section, so this sits at the hips. The garter stitch section has a looser tension, and this makes the yarn behave differently, draping beautifully over the body. Once again, there is no need to do any shaping – these stitches do all the work for you.

The *Huggable hoodie* (pages 98–103) has a honeycomb cable stitch pattern. This is my favourite stitch when worked in merino wool; I love the texture it creates. I chose this stitch pattern because it almost creates a double-layer fibre, which I thought was perfect for a hoodie to keep you warm in crisp, cold weather. It also creates a stretchy knitted fabric, so is comfortable and flattering to everyone who wears it.

> *"No matter how long you've been knitting, you can always find a new stitch to use."*

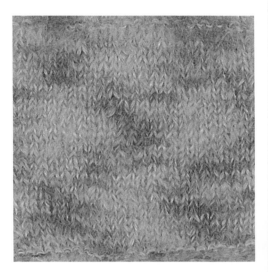

The Kimono-sleeved smock *features an intricate cable pattern at the top that fits closely to the body, then switches to stockinette switch to elegantly drape over the hips.*

The On the button tank top *is made mostly in stretchy garter stitch fabric that skims loosely over the body. The pretty lacy section at the hem has a tighter tension and fits closely over the hips and bottom.*

Projects

Ruffled up vest top

This top takes a basic vest top shape and transforms it with a wealth of feminine flourishes.

> " *Mohair is a very feminine yarn; light, fluffy, hazy and cuddly. Here I've used a variegated yarn in pretty pastel colours.* "

This is a garment that will make you revel in your femininity. The ribbing over the bust fits closely to shapely curves, while the ruffle trim at the hem adds a frothy, flirty touch. The subtle empire line lengthens the torso, while the delicate lacy pattern used for the main body of the vest top has plenty of stretch so will skim over your body without looking clumpy.

For extra glamour and sparkle, I've added a border of knitted-in beads around the deep V-neck, to show off your cleavage. The keyhole neckline is fastened with a shiny flower-shaped button and beaded button loop. Make the most of pretty details by choosing trimmings that enhance the colours in the yarn.

measurements

to fit chest	extra small	small	medium	large	extra large
	32–34in	34–36in	38–40in	40–42in	44–46in
	81.5–86.5cm	86.5–91.5cm	96.5–101.5cm	101.5–106.5cm	112–117cm
actual measurement	35in	37¾in	40¾in	43½in	46¼in
	89cm	96cm	103.5cm	110.5cm	118cm
length	25½in	26¼in	27¼in	28¼in	29¼in
	65cm	67cm	69cm	72cm	74cm

materials

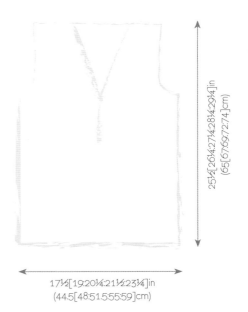

25½[26¼:27¼:28¼:29¼]in
(65[67:69:72:74]cm)

17½[19:20¼:21½:23¼]in
(44.5[48:51.5:55:59]cm)

- 6[7:7:8:8] x ⅞oz (25g) balls of light-weight (DK) mohair (79% mohair, 21% nylon; 115yd/105m per ball) *(photographed in Louisa Harding La Salute Quattro, shade 2 Berry, Rose, Aqua, Turquoise)*
- Pair of size 8 (5mm) needles
- Pair of size 6 (4mm) needles
- Stitch holders
- 184[194:204:218:228] beads

gauge

22sts and 30 rows to 4in (10cm) square over st st using size 8 (5mm) needles

A narrow band of garter stitch separates the ribbed bust from the lacy lower section of the top. This creates a flattering empire-line waist effect, enhancing the bust and lengthening the torso.

" *The difference in stitches is very dramatic with the mohair. The ribbing is very solid, while the lace gracefully floats around the waist* "

back

With size 8 (5mm) needles, cast on 242[262:282:302:322]sts.

1st row (right side): p2, [k8, p2]to end.

2nd row: k2, [p8, k2]to end.

3rd row: p2, [ybk, s1, k1, psso, k4, k2tog, p2]to end. 194[210:226:242:258]sts.

4th row: k2, [k6, p2]to end.

5th row: p2, [ybk, s1, k1, psso, k2, k2tog, p2]to end. 146[158:170:182:194]sts.

6th row: k2, [k4, p2]to end.

7th row: p2, [ybk, s1, k1, psso, k2tog, p2]to end. 98[106:114:122:130]sts.

Knit 3 rows.

1st rib row: k2, [p2, k2]to end.

2nd rib row: p2, [k2, p2]to end.

These 2 rows form the rib patt.

Rep the last 2 rows once more.

Knit 3 rows.

1st patt row (right side): p2, [k3, p1]to end.

2nd patt row: [k1, p3] to last 2sts, k2.

3rd patt row: as **1st** patt row.

4th patt row: [k1, yrn, p3tog, yrn]to last 2sts, k2.

5th patt row: k3, p1, [k3, p1]to last 2sts, k2.

6th patt row: p2, k1, [p3, k1]to last 3sts, p3.

7th patt row: as **5th** patt row.

8th patt row: p2tog, yrn, k1, yrn, [p3tog, yrn, k1, yrn]to last 3sts, p2tog, p1.

These 8 rows form the lace patt.

Rep the last 8 rows until back measures 11¾in (30cm) from cast-on edge, ending with a **right side** row.

Knit 3 rows.

Starting with a **1st rib row**, cont in rib until back measures 17½[17¾:18:19:19¾]in (44[45:46:48:50]cm) from cast-on edge, ending with a **wrong side** row.

shape armholes

Bind off 4sts at the beg of the next 2 rows. 90[98:106:114:122]sts.

Dec row: k2, k2togtbl, rib to last 4sts, k2tog, k2.

This row sets the position of the dec.

Dec one st as set above at each end of 3 foll 4th rows. 82[90:98:106:114]sts.

Starting with a **1st rib row**, cont without shaping in rib patt until armhole measures 8¼[8¾:9:9½:9½]in (21[22:23:24:24]cm) from start of armhole shaping, ending with a **wrong side** row.

shape shoulders

Bind off 21[24:27:30:33]sts at the beg of the next 2 rows.

Leave rem 40[42:44:46:48]sts on a holder.

The ribbed section at the top half of the vest top will fit smoothly over the bust for a good fit.

As a pretty finishing touch, I've suggested making a buttonloop from the beads and sewing on a complementary button. See page 120 for full instructions on how to do this.

front

Work as given for the back until front measures 11¾in [30cm] from cast-on edge, ending with a **right side** row.

Knit 3 rows.

shape left side

Next row: [k2, p2] until there are 44[48:52:56:60]sts on right-hand needle, k5, slip rem sts on a holder, turn and patt to end. 49[53:57:61:65]sts.

1st patt row (wrong side): p5, [k2, p2]to end.

2nd patt row (right side): [k2, p2]to last 5sts, knit to end.

These 2 rows form the rib patt with 5sts neck edge.

Rep the last 2 rows until front measures 17½[17¾:18:19:19¾]in (44[45:46:48:50]cm) from cast-on edge, ending with **wrong side** row.

shape armhole and left neck

Cast off 4sts at the beg of the next row. 46 [49:53:57:61] sts.

Work one row.

Next row: k2, k2togtbl, rib to last 6sts, k2tog, k2, p2. 44 [47:51:55:59] sts.

This row sets the position of the dec sts.

Dec one st as above at armhole edge of 3 foll alt rows **at the same time** dec one st at neck edge of every foll alt row until there are 21[24:27:30:33]sts.

Cont without shaping in rib patt, until armhole measures 8¼[8¾:9:9½:9½]in (21[22:23:24:24]cm) from start of armhole shaping, ending with a **wrong side** row.

Bind off.

shape armhole and right neck

With right side facing, rejoin yarn to rem 49[53:57:61:65]sts

Complete to match left side and neck, reversing shapings.

edging

Join shoulder seams. Thread beads onto yarn. With right side facing and size 6 (4mm) needles, pick up and knit 72[76:80:86:90]sts up right front neck, knit 40[42:44:46:48]sts from holder at centre back, pick up and knit 72[76:80:86:90]sts down left front neck. 184[194:204:218:228]sts.

Bind off, sliding a bead up next to each st as you bind off.

to make up

Join side seams. If desired, make button loop and attach button as described on page 120.

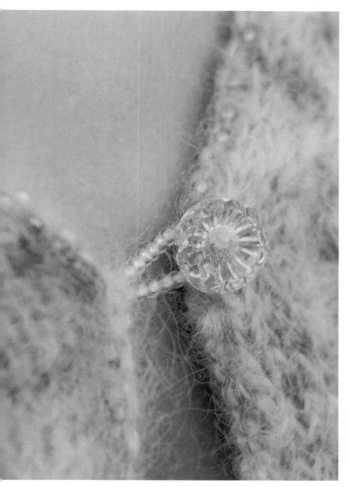

"*The deep V-neck is a flattering look on most body shapes whether you're buxom or smaller-busted, and has the slimming effect of making your neck look longer.*"

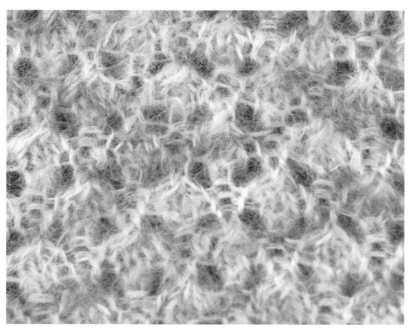

Look again...

With this variation, I simplified the garment by leaving out the beaded neck edging and the bottom edge ruffled trim. However, the delicate pink shade still makes this top look very pretty and feminine.

materials

- ☀ 6[7:7:8:8] x 1¾oz (50g) balls of light-weight (DK) cotton (100% organic cotton; 120yd/110m per ball)
  (photographed in Mirasol Sampa, 614 Lychee)
- ☀ Pair of size 5 (3.75mm) needles
- ☀ Stitch holders

Gauge and measurements are as for main garment but using size 5 (3.75mm) needles instead.

back

With size 5 (3.75mm) needles, cast on 98(106:114:122:130)sts.
1st rib row: k2, [p2, k2]to end.
2nd rib row: p2, [k2, p2]to end.
These 2 rows form the rib patt.
Rep the last 2 rows once more.
1st patt row (right side): p2, [k3, p1]to end.
2nd patt row: [k1, p3] to last 2sts, k2.
3rd patt row: as **1st patt row.**
4th patt row: [k1, yrn, p3tog, yrn]to last 2sts, k2.
5th patt row: k3, p1, [k3, p1]to last 2sts, k2.
6th patt row: p2, k1, [p3, k1]to last 3sts, p3.
7th patt row: as **5th patt row.**
8th patt row: p2tog, yrn, k1, yrn, [p3tog, yrn, k1, yrn]to last 3sts, p2tog, p1.
These 8 rows form the lace patt.
Rep the last 8 rows until back measures 11¾in (30cm)from cast on edge, ending with a **right side** row.
Knit 3 rows.
Starting with a **1st rib row,** cont in rib until back measures 17½[17¾:18:19:19¾]in (44[45:46:48:50]cm) from cast on edge, ending with a wrong side row.

shape armholes

Bind off 4sts at the beg of the next 2 rows. 90(98:106:114:122)sts
Dec row: k2, k2togtbl, rib to last 4sts, k2tog, k2.
This row sets the position of the dec.
Dec one st as set above at each end of 3 foll 4th rows.

82(90:98:106:114)sts.
Starting with a **1st rib row,** cont without shaping in rib patt until armhole measures 8¼[8¾:9:9½:9½]in (21[22:23:24:24]cm) from start of armhole shaping, ending with a **wrong side** row.

shape shoulders

Bind off 21(24:27:30:33)sts at the beg of the next 2 rows.
Leave rem 40(42:44:46:48)sts on a holder.

front

Work as given for the back until front measures 17½[17¾:18:19:19¾]in (44[45:46:48:50]cm) from cast-on edge, ending with a **wrong side** row.

shape armhole and left neck

Next row: bind off 4sts, patt until there are 46 (49:53:57:61) sts.
Work one row.
Next row: k2, k2togtbl, rib to last 6sts, k2tog, k2, p2. 44 (47:51:55:59) sts
This row sets the position of the dec sts.
Dec one st as above at armhole edge of 3 foll alt rows **at the same time** dec one st at neck edge of every foll alt row until there are 21(24:27:30:33)sts.
Cont without shaping in rib patt, until armhole measures 8¼[8¾:9:9½:9½]in (21[22:23:24:24]cm) from start of armhole shaping, ending with a **wrong side** row.
Bind off.

shape armhole and right side

With right side facing, rejoin yarn to rem 49sts, patt to end.
Bind off 4sts at the beg of the next row. 46sts
Work as given for left neck.
Complete as given for the left side and neck, reversing shapings.
off sliding a bead up next to each st as you cast off.

to make up

Join shoulder seams. Join side seams.

On the button tank top

This garment plays with the traditional tank-top shape; the addition of a lacy panel and some flirty buttons give it a completely different feminine look.

The main body of this tank top is knitted in garter stitch. This creates a forgiving fabric that is stretchy and fluid. It will drape and skim over your figure rather than clinging and bunching. Garter stitch can look a bit bulky, but here I used a fine-weight (4ply) yarn so the fabric is relatively fine. This is a fairly loose-fitting item; the details of the fun buttons on the shoulder straps and the lace panelling at the bottom add pretty touches for feminine appeal.

This is a longer-length top, and the eye will be drawn to the lace edging at the hip, thereby creating the effect of a lengthened torso. The simple squared-off neckline frames the face and neck attractively.

"Merino is a classic knitting yarn: it is fine, soft, smooth, slightly lustrous and offers very even stitch definition. I've used a yarn with a subtly variegated colour in a warm neutral shade."

measurements

to fit chest	extra small	small	medium	large	extra large
	32–34in	36–38in	40–42in	42–44in	46–48in
	81.5–86.5cm	91.5–96.5cm	101.5–106.5cm	106.5–112cm	117–122cm
actual measurement	38¼in	42¼in	44¼in	46¼in	50¼in
	97.5cm	107.5cm	112.5cm	117.5cm	127.5cm
length (excluding straps)	21¼in	21½in	22in	22¾in	23½in54cm
	54cm	55cm	56cm	58cm	60cm

materials

- 4[4:5:5:5] x 3½oz (100g) balls of fine-weight (4ply) merino wool (100% merino; 320yd/293m per ball) *(photographed in Colinette Jitterbug, Dali shade 161 Oyster Blush)*
- Pair of size 3 (3.25mm) needles
- Pair of size 3 (2.75mm) needles
- Stitch holders
- 4 buttons

gauge

24sts and 40 rows to 4in (10cm) square over g st using size 3 (3.25mm) needles

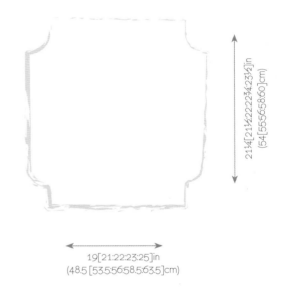

21¼[21½:22:22¾:23½]in
(54[55:56:58:60]cm)

19[21:22:23:25]in
(48.5 [53.5:56:58.5:63.5]cm)

While you are knitting the lace section, or when the garment is lying flat, you won't really see the full effect of the lacy pattern. It's only when the tank top is worn and the lace panel is stretched out that you will see it in its full glory.

"*I love the way the patterning of the lace creates a vertical line that draws your eye up the garment.*"

back

With size 2 (2.75mm) needles, cast on 117[129:135:141:153]sts.

1st, 2nd and 3rd patt rows: knit to end.

4th patt row (right side): k2, [yrn, k1, s1, k2tog, psso, k1, yrn, k1]to last st, k1.

5th patt row: purl to end.

6th patt row: as 4th patt row.

7th patt row: as 5th patt row.

8th patt row: as 4th patt row.

These 8 rows form the lace patt.

Rep the last 8 rows until work measures 4¾in (12cm) from cast-on edge, ending with a 8th patt row.

Change to size 3 (3.25mm) needles.

Starting with a knit row, cont in g st until work measures 18[18½:19:19¾:20½]in (46[47:48:50:52]cm) from cast-on edge, ending with a wrong side row.

shape armholes

Bind off 5sts at beg of next 2 rows. 107[119:125:131:143]sts.

Dec row: k3, k2togtbl, knit to last 5sts, k2tog, k3.

105[117:123:129:141]sts.

This row sets the position of the dec.

Dec 1 st at each end as set above of next 5 foll 4th rows, ending with a right side row. 95[107:113:119:131]sts.

Work 15 rows.

shape right strap

Bind off 16[16:18:18:20]sts, knit 14[14:16:18:18]sts, leave rem sts on a holder, turn.

Cont to knit on these 14sts until strap measures 11in (28cm), ending with a wrong side row.

Buttonhole row: k3, k2tog, yrn, k4, yrn, k2tog, k3.

Knit 5 rows.

Bind off.

If you prefer a more classic, streamlined neck, you could omit the buttons and buttonholes on the shoulder straps and simply sew the plain strap into place, making the back the front and therefore sewing the strap at the back.

shape left strap

With right side facing, rejoin yarn to rem sts, bind off 35[47:45:47:55]sts, knit to end.

Bind off 16(16:18:18:20)sts, knit to end.

Work to match right strap.

front

Work as given for back until there are 95[107:113:119:131]sts, ending with a right side row.

Work 9 rows.

Strap slits bind-off row (right side): knit 17[17:19:19:21]sts, bind off 12[12:14:16:16]sts, knit until there are 37(49:47:49:57)sts after bind-off, bind off 12[12:14:16:16]sts, knit to end.

Strap slits cast-on row: knit to end, casting on 12 (12:14:16:16) sts over those bound off on previous row.

Work 4 rows.

Bind off.

to make up

Join side seams. Position and sew buttons into place.

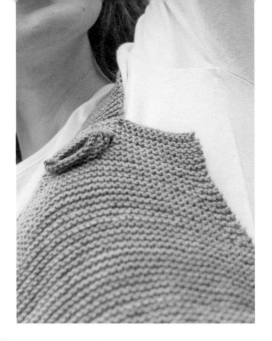

" The delicate variegation of the yarn and the lace pattern transforms this simple shape into something very feminine."

Two-yarn tunic

This chic hip-length tunic features a flattering empire-line waist and an elegant A-line shape.

> " *A fine, fluffy mohair yarn held together with a crisp linen ribbon yarn creates a unique and tactile fabric.* "

This is a simple knit; the back and front are both knitted to the same shape and then seamed together. The main body is knitted in stockinette stitch with no shaping; the A-line silhouette is created simply by changing the needle size. A ridge of garter stitch creates the effect of an empire-line waist. As this falls under the bust rather than at your natural waist, it creates a slimming look, drawing the eye to the narrowest part of the torso. This longer-length tunic gently skims the hips rather than clinging to them. The chic silhouette is finished off with a neat square neckline to frame your neck and face.

The combination of the two yarns in similar but not identical shades of blue creates a subtle and appealing two-tone effect. This is a very tactile fabric, combining the warmth and fuzziness of the mohair with the crisp, structured linen ribbon.

measurements

to fit chest	extra small	small	medium	large	extra large
	32–34in	34–36in	38–40in	40–42in	44–46in
	81.5–86.5 cm	86.5–91.5 cm	96.5–101.5 cm	101.5–106.5 cm	112–117cm
actual measurement	33½in	37¼in	41in	43¼in	47¼in
	85.5cm	95cm	104.5cm	110cm	120cm
length	31in	31in	32½in	32½in	34¼in
	79cm	79 cm	83 cm	83 cm	87cm

materials

- Yarn **A**: 2[2:3:3:4] x 1¾oz (50g) hanks of linen paper ribbon (100% linen; 280yd/250m per hank)
- Yarn **B**: 3[3:3:4:4] x ⅞oz (25g) hanks of fine-weight mohair (70% kid mohair, 30% polyamide; 242yd/221m per hank)
  (photographed in (A) Habu Shosenshi Linen Paper, shade 120 Indigo and (B) Colinette Parisienne, shade 118 Velvet Damson)
- Pair of size 8 (5mm) needles
- Pair of size 6 (4mm) needles
- Pair of size 5 (3.75mm) needles
- Stitch holders

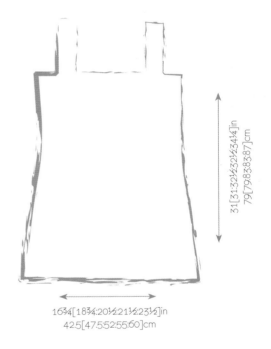

31[31:32½:32½:34¼]in
79[79:83:83:87]cm

16¾[18¾:20½:21½:23½]in
42.5[47.5:52:55:60]cm

gauge

21sts and 32 rows to 4in (10cm) square over st st using size 5 (3.75mm) needles and one strand of yarn **A** and one strand of yarn **B** held together

This pattern could easily be adapted to be knitted on a circular needle if you prefer to create a seamless garment. This could enhance the garment's flattering, fluid shape. Knit in one piece to the armholes and then knit the front and back pieces separately once you need to shape for the straps.

" *You will be working with two yarns held together throughout. Make sure you pick up the two strands for each stitch you make; it's easy to miss one when working with more than one yarn.* "

back and front alike

With size 8 (5mm) needles and yarn **B** only, cast on
90[100:110:116:126]sts.
Knit one row.
Using one strand of yarn **A** and one strand of yarn **B** throughout,
starting with a **knit** row, cont in st st until work measures 17¾in
(45cm) from cast-on edge, ending with a **right side** row.
Change to size 6 (4mm) needles.
Knit 3 rows.
Change to size 5 (3.75mm) needles.
Starting with a **knit** row, cont in st st until work measures
23½[23½:24½:24½:25¼]in (60[60:62:62:64]cm) from cast-on edge,
ending with a **wrong side** row.

*You can move the empire-line effect (created by knitting 3
rows to create a garter-stitch ridge) up or down so it fits
right underneath your bust or a little lower down, depending
on the size of your bust and what look will flatter you most.*

shape straps

Next row: p14[14:16:16:18], k15, p32[42:48:54:66], k15,
p14[14:16:16:18].
Next row: Bind off 14[14:16:16:18]sts knitwise, p14,
k32[42:48:54:66], p15, knit to end.
Next row: Bind off 14[14:16:16:18]sts purlwise, knit until there are
15[15:16:17:18]sts, turn and leave rem sts on a holder.
Cont without shaping in st st on the 15[15:16:17:18]sts until strap
measures 7½[7½:8¼:8¼:9]in (19[19:21:21:23]cm) from start of
armhole shaping, ending with a **wrong side** row. Bind off.
With right side facing, leave centre 32[42:48:54:66]sts on a holder,
rejoin yarn to 15[15:16:17:18]sts, work to match other strap.

to make up

Join strap edges. Join side seams.

> 66 *This tunic's gentle A-line shape will flatter your figure whether you are a curvy pear-shape or a beanpole.* 99

Look again...

This variation garment is knitted in a single yarn, a cotton and linen blend. The main change in the design is the simple yet effective addition of an eyelet row under the bust, set off with a ribbon tie. This changes a basic A-line tunic into a subtly feminine top, as more attention is drawn to the empire-line waist and consequently to the bust.

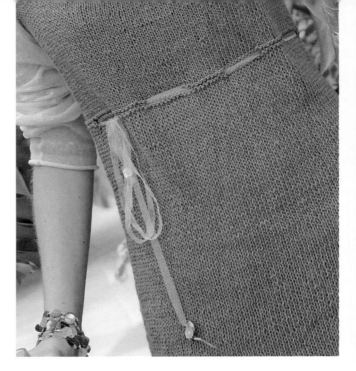

materials

- ☀ 9[10:10:11:11] x 1¾oz (50g) balls of cotton and linen blend (53% cotton, 47% linen; 122yd/111m per ball)
  (photographed in Katia Linen, shade 13 Gray)
- ☀ Pair of size 8 (5mm) needles
- ☀ Pair of size 6 (4mm) needles
- ☀ Pair of size 5 (3.75mm) needles
- ☀ Stitch holders
- ☀ Length of ribbon
- ☀ Buttons to decorate ribbon (optional)

Gauge and measurements are as for main garment. Note that in this variation only one strand is used throughout.

back and front alike

With size 8 (5mm) needles, cast on 90[100:110:116:126]sts.
Starting with a **knit** row, cont in st st until work measures 17¾in (45cm) from cast-on edge, ending with a **right side** row.
Change to size 6 (4mm) needles.
Knit one row.
Eyelet row: [k4, yrn, k2tog, k4] to end.
Knit one row.
Change to size 5 (3.75mm) needles.
Starting with a **knit** row, cont in st st until work measures 23½[23½:24½:24½:25¼]in (60[60:62:62:64]cm) from cast-on edge, ending with a **wrong side** row.

shape straps

Next row: p14[14:16:16:18], k15, p32[42:48:54:66], k15, p14[14:16:16:18].
Next row: Bind off 14[14:16:16:18]sts knitwise, p14, k32[42:48:54:66], p15, knit to end.

> *" The use of a more traditional mix of fibres – cotton and linen – creates a more practical garment, while the addition of the ribbon tie keeps a feminine feel."*

Next row: Bind off 14[14:16:16:18]sts purlwise, knit until there are 15[15:16:17:18]sts, turn and leave rem sts on a holder.
Cont without shaping in st st on the 15[15:16:17:18]sts until strap measures 7½[7½:8¼:8¼:9]in (19[19:21:21:23]cm) from start of armhole shaping, ending with a **wrong side** row.
Bind off.
With right side facing, leave centre 32[42:48:54:66]sts on a holder, rejoin yarn to 15[15:16:17:18]sts, work to match other strap.

to make up

Join strap edges. Join side seams.
Thread ribbon through eyelets. To make an interesting detail, I threaded buttons onto the end of the ribbon.

Silver shimmer shrug

This cropped shrug with elbow-length sleeves is a versatile garment that will give you an instant glamour boost.

66 *I chose a ribbon yarn that combines a duller gunmetal silver with a sharper, brighter metallic thread for a fabric that shimmers.* 99

Ribbon yarn can be a little loose and sloppy-looking if knitted in stockinette stitch, so I used a basketstitch pattern for the body of the shrug to give the fabric some heft and structure. This stitch pattern is also quite stretchy, so the knitted fabric will hug your shape.

Metallic yarn is the perfect choice for glamorous eveningwear, teamed with an elegant dress, but it looks funky and edgy in the daytime, worn with jeans. The cropped length is also versatile; you can choose what to wear under the shrug depending on how much you want to show off – throw it over a slinky vest top if you're feeling daring, or layer it with a long-sleeved jersey top for more coverage.

measurements

to fit chest	extra small	small	medium	large	extra large
	32–34in	34–36in	36–38in	38–40in	40–42in
	81.5–86.5cm	86.5–91.5cm	91.5–96.5cm	96.5–101.5cm	101.5–106.5cm
actual measurement	33½in	36½in	39¼in	42¼in	45in
	85cm	92.5cm	100cm	107cm	114.5cm
length	18in	18in	19¾in	19¾in	20½in
	46cm	46cm	50cm	50cm	52cm
sleeve length	7in	7in	7in	7in	7in
	18cm	18cm	18cm	18cm	18cm

materials

- ❋ 9[10:10:11:11] x 1¾oz (50g) balls of light-weight (DK) metallic ribbon yarn (97% nylon, 3% polyester; 93yd/85m per ball) *(photographed in Louisa Harding Glisten, shade 28 Silver)*
- ❋ Pair of size 8 (5mm) knitting needles
- ❋ Ribbon for tie

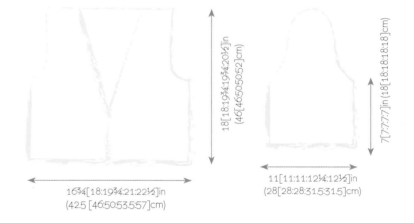

18[18:19¾:19¾:20½]in (46[46:50:50:52]cm)

16¾[18:19¾:21:22½]in (42.5 [46:50:53.5:57]cm)

7[7:7:7:7]in (18[18:18:18:18]cm)

11[11:11:12¼:12½]in (28[28:28:31.5:31.5]cm)

gauge

22sts and 32 rows to 4in (10cm) square over patt using size 8 (5mm) needles

back

With size 8 (5mm) needles, cast on 94[102:110:118:126]sts.
Knit 2 rows.
Eyelet row (right side): k2, [yrn, k2tog]to last 2sts, k2.
Knit one row.
1st patt row (right side): knit to end.
2nd patt row: purl to end.
3rd patt row: k2, [p2, k2]to end.
4th patt row: p2, [k2, p2]to end.
5th patt row: knit to end.
6th patt row: purl to end.
7th patt row: as 4th patt row.
8th patt row: as 3rd patt row.
These 8 rows form stitch patt.
Rep the last 8 rows until back measures 9½[9½:10¼:10¼:11]in (24[24:26:26:28]cm) from cast-on edge, ending with a **wrong side** row.

" This shrug's cropped length makes it versatile and flattering to a wide variety of body shapes. If you're willowy, just slip it over a camisole or vest top. If you want more coverage, wear it over a favourite dress."

shape armholes

Bind off 5sts at the beg of the next 2 rows. 84[92:100:108:116]sts.
Dec one st at each end of next and 4 foll 4th rows.
74[82:90:98:106]sts.
Keeping patt correct, cont without shaping until armhole measures 8½[8½:9½:9½:9½]in (22[22:24:24:24]cm) from start of armhole shaping, ending with a **wrong side** row.

shape shoulders

Bind off 19[23:26:30:33]sts at the beg of the next 2 rows.
Bind off rem 36[36:38:38:40]sts.

left front

With size 8 (5mm) needles, cast on 47[51:55:59:63]sts.
Knit 2 rows.
Eyelet row (right side): k2, [yrn, k2tog]to last st, k1.
Knit one row.
1st patt row (right side): knit to end.
2nd patt row: k3, purl to end.
3rd patt row: [k2, p2]to last 3sts, k3.
4th patt row: k3, [k2, p2]to end.
5th patt row: knit to end.
6th patt row: k3, purl to end.
7th patt row: [p2, k2]to last 3sts, k3.
8th patt row: k3, [p2, k2]to end.
These 8 rows form the stitch patt.
Rep the last 8 rows until left front measures 4¾in (12cm) from cast-on edge, ending with a **right side** row.

The garter-stitch edging of the neckline is worked at the same time as the main left and right fronts (as opposed to being picked up and worked later). The V-shaped neck is flattering on most people, giving shape to slender frames and enhancing the curves of fuller-figured women.

shape neck

Dec one st at neck edge on the next and every foll 4th row until left front measures 9½[9½:10¼:10¼:11]in (24[24:26:26:28]cm) from cast-on edge, ending with a **wrong side** row.
Keeping patt correct, cont to dec one st at neck edge on every foll 4th row shaping armhole as folls at the same time:

shape armhole

Bind off 5sts at the beg of the next row.
Work one row.
Dec one st at armhole edge of next and 4 foll 4th rows.
Keeping patt correct, cont to dec one st at neck edge until there are 19[23:26:30:33]sts.
Cont without shaping in patt, until armhole measures 8½[8½:9½:9½:9½]in (22[22:24:24:24]cm) from start of armhole shaping, ending with a **wrong side** row.
Bind off.

right front

With size 8 (5mm) needles, cast on 47[51:55:59:63]sts.
Knit 2 rows.
Eyelet row (right side): k1, [k2tog, yrn]to last 2sts, k2.
Knit one row.
1st patt row (right side): knit to end.
2nd patt row: purl to last 3sts, k3.
3rd patt row: k3, [k2, p2]to end.
4th patt row: [k2, p2]to last 3sts, k3.
5th patt row: knit to end.
6th patt row: purl to last 3sts, k3.
7th patt row: k3, [p2, k2]to end.
8th patt row: [p2, k2]to last 3sts, k3.
These 8 rows form the stitch patt.
Work to match left front, reversing shapings.

sleeves

With size 8 (5mm) needles, cast on 62[62:62:70:70]sts.
Work as given for the back until sleeve measures 7in (18cm) from cast-on edge, ending with a **wrong side** row.

shape top

Bind off 5sts at the beg of the next 2 rows. 52[52:52:60:60]sts.
Dec one st at each end of next and 6 foll 4th rows. 38[38:38:46:46]sts.
Work one row.
Dec one st at each end of next and 4 foll alt rows. 28[28:28:36:36]sts.
Work 1[1:3:3:3] row(s).
Dec one st at each end of next and every foll row until 10[10:6:6:6]sts rem.
Bind off.

The sleeves also feature eyelets around the bottom edge. Here I've chosen not to thread ribbon through, but you could do this if you wanted to dress the shrug up more.

to make up

Join shoulder seams. Sew on sleeves, placing centre of sleeves to shoulder seams. Join side and sleeve seams. Thread a length of ribbon through the eyelets at the bottom edge for the tie.

This shrug works just as well without the ribbon tie, if you prefer to wear it hanging open. The V-neck shaping means it will still fit well over the bust and then fall in a flattering drape.

Lace-edged wrapover

This versatile short-sleeved wrapover top is knitted in stretchy garter stitch and embellished with pretty lace edgings.

> " *Baby llama is a very warm and quite solid yarn, so works perfectly for smaller garments. It is soft and somewhat fluffy, with long fibres that create a soft and hazy look.* "

Stylish women have long known about the magic of a wrapover top to fit and flatter, whatever your shape. They are one of those miraculous garments that seem to suit everyone, from the skinny to the voluptuous. This one features a deep V-neck that will lengthen your torso, while the cropped length enhances the waist. Garter stitch fabric is also remarkably forgiving because of its stretch and drape; it will skim over the body without clinging to it.

Wrapover tops are very feminine-looking, and here I've enhanced the romantic look by adding lace edgings to the sleeves and the waist. These edgings are knitted separately and then sewn into place.

Shawl-collar cardigan

This vibrant emerald-green cardigan features a flattering vertical stitch pattern combining ribbing with a mock cable stitch.

The vivid jewel colour of this cardigan creates tremendous style impact. The cardigan features an allover stitch pattern of vertical lines. This creates a slimming effect, elongating the torso and drawing the eye down the body. The elegantly draping shawl collar is made by picking up stitches along the sides and neck of the garment. The collar is shaped to create a gentle curved shape that will set off your neck and face perfectly.

The stitch pattern on the body of the cardigan is carried through to the sleeves. Three-quarter-length sleeves are always an elegant choice; they draw attention to the narrowest part of the arm and make arms look longer and slimmer.

"Bamboo yarn has a wonderfully smooth and lustrous texture. It creates a very fluid knitted fabric that will drape in a flattering way."

measurements

to fit chest	extra small	small	medium	large	extra large
	32-34	36-38	40-42	42-44	46-48in
	81.5-86.5cm	91.5-96.5cm	101.5-106.5cm	106.5-112cm	117-122cm
actual measurements	36½in	40in	43¼in	46½in	49¾in
	93cm	101.5cm	110cm	118cm	126.5cm
length	22½in	22½in	22½in	23¼in	23¼in
	57cm	57cm	57cm	59cm	59cm
sleeve length	10¼in	10¼in	10¼in	10¼in	10¼in
	26cm	26cm	26cm	26cm	26cm

materials

- 11[11:12:12:13] x 1¾oz (50g) balls of light-weight (DK) bamboo yarn (80% bamboo, 20% extra-fine merino; 116yd/106m per ball) *(photographed in Debbie Bliss Prima, shade 15 Jade)*
- Pair of size 6 (4mm) needles
- Pair of size 5 (3.75mm) needles
- Stitch holders
- 1 button

gauge

24sts and 32 rows to 4in (10cm) square over patt when slightly stretched using size 6 (4mm) needles

special instructions

C2B: miss the first stitch on the left-hand needle and knit into the front of the second stitch. Do not slip the worked stitch off the needle, but knit into the front of the first stitch (the 'missed stitch'). Slip both the stitches off the needle together.
C2F: knit the second stitch on the left-hand needle through the back, working behind the first stitch. Then knit into the front of the first stitch. Slip both the stitches off the needle together.

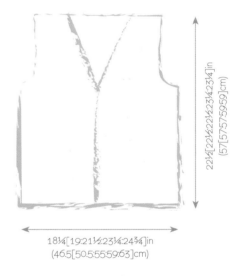

22½[22½:22½:23¼:23¼]in (57[57:57:59:59]cm)

18¼[19:21½:23¼:24¾]in (46.5[50.5:55:59:63]cm)

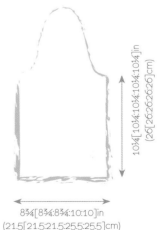

10¼[10¼:10¼:10¼:10¼]in (26[26:26:26:26]cm)

8¾[8¾:8¾:10:10]in (21.5[21.5:21.5:25.5:25.5]cm)

back

With size 6 (4mm) needles, cast on 112[122:132:142:152]sts.
1st row: k2, [p2, k4, p2, k2]to end.
2nd row: p2, [k2, p4, k2, p2] to end.
1st patt row (right side): k2, [p2, C2B, C2Fp2, k2]to end.
2nd and 4th patt row: p2, [k2, p4, k2, p2] to end.
3rd patt row: k2, [p2, C2FC2B, p2, k2]to end.
These 4 rows form the patt.
Rep the last 4 rows until back measures 13¾in (35cm) from cast-on edge, ending with a **wrong side** row.

shape armholes

Bind off 5sts at the beg of the next 2 rows. 102[112:122:132:142]sts.
Dec one st at each end of next and 4 foll 4th rows.
92[102:112:122:132]sts.
Cont without shaping in patt until armhole measures 8¾[8¾:8¾:9½:9½]in (22[22:22:24:24]cm) from start of armhole shaping, ending with a **wrong side** row.

shape shoulders

Bind off 26[29:32:35:39]sts at the beg of the next 2 rows.
Leave rem centre 40[44:48:52:54]sts on a holder.

left front

With size 6 (4mm) needles, cast on 53[58:63:68:73]sts.
1st row:, k0(2:0:2:0), p0(2:0:2:0), [k2, p2, k4, p2]to last 3(4:3:4:3)sts, knit to end.
2nd row: p3(4:3:4:3), [k2, p4, k2, p2]to last 0(4:0:4:0)sts, k0(2:0:2:0), p0(2:0:2:0).
1st patt row (right side): k0(2:0:2:0), p0(2:0:2:0), [k2, p2, C2B, C2Fp2]to last 3(4:3:4:3)sts, knit to end.
2nd and 4th patt row: p3, [k2, p4, k2, p2] to end.
3rd patt row: k0(2:0:2:0), p0(2:0:2:0), [k2, p2, C2FC2B, p2]to last 3(4:3:4:3)sts, knit to end.
These 4 rows form the patt.
Rep the last 4 rows until left front measures 13¾in (35cm) from cast-on edge, ending with a **wrong side** row.

shape armhole and neck

Bind off 5sts at the beg of next row. 48[53:58:63:68]sts.
Knit one row.
Keeping patt correct, dec one st at armhole edge of next and 4 foll 4th rows **at the same time** dec one st at neck edge of next and every foll alt row until there are 26[29:32:35:39]sts.
Cont without shaping in patt until armhole measures 8¾[8¾:8¾:9½:9½]in (22[22:22:24:24]cm) from start of armhole shaping, ending with a **wrong side** row.
Bind off.

right front

With size 6 (4mm) needles, cast on 53[58:63:68:73]sts.
1st row: k3(4:3:4:3), [p2, k4, p2, k2]to last 0(4:0:4:0)sts, p0(2:0:2:0), k0(2:0:2:0).
2nd row: p0(2:0:2:0), k0(2:0:2:0) [p2, k2, p4, k2] to last 3(4:3:4:3)sts, purl to end.
1st patt row (right side): k3(4:3:4:3), [p2, C2B, C2Fp2, k2]to last 0(4:0:4:0)sts, p0(2:0:2:0), k0(2:0:2:0).
2nd and 4th patt row: p0(2:0:2:0), k0(2:0:2:0), [p2, k2, p4, k2]to last 3(4:3:4:3)sts, purl to end.
3rd patt row: k3(4:3:4:3)sts, [p2, C2FC2B, p2, k2]to last 0(4:0:4:0)sts, p0(2:0:2:0), k0(2:0:2:0).
These 4 rows form the patt.
Work to match left front, reversing shapings.

sleeves

With size 6 (4mm) needles, cast on 62[62:62:72:72]sts.
Starting with a **1st patt row**, work as given for the back, then cont in patt as given for the back until sleeve measures 10¼in (26cm) from cast-on edge, ending with a **wrong side** row.

shape top

Bind off 5sts at the beg of the next 2 rows. 52[52:52:62:62]sts.
Dec one st at each end of next and 7 foll 4th rows. 36[36:36:46:46]sts.
Work 5 rows.
Dec one st at each end of next and 6 foll alt rows. 22[22:22:32:32]sts.
Work one row.
Bind off rem sts.

collar

Join shoulder seams. With right side facing and size 5 (3.75mm) needles, pick up and knit 129[129:129:133:133]sts up right neck, knit 40[44:48:52:54]sts from holder at centre back, pick up and knit 129[129:129:133:133]sts down left front neck. 298[302:306:318:322]sts.
1st rib row (wrong side): p2, [k2, p2]to end.
2nd rib row: k2, [p2, k2]to end.
These 2 rows form the rib patt.
Work these 2 rows once only.

shape shawl collar

Next row: rib 169[173:177:185:187]sts, turn.
Next row: rib 40[44:48:52:54]sts, turn.
Next row: rib 44[48:52:56:58]sts, turn.
Next row: rib 48[52:56:60:62]sts, turn.
Next row: rib 52[56:60:64:66]sts, turn.
Next row: rib 56[60:64:68:70]sts, turn.
Next row: rib 60[64:68:72:74]sts, turn.
Next row: rib 64[68:72:76:78]sts, turn.
Next row: rib 68[72:76:80:82]sts, turn.

Next row: rib 72[76:80:84:86]sts, turn.
Next row: rib 76[80:84:88:90]sts, turn.
Next row: rib 80[84:88:92:94]sts, turn.
Next row: rib 84[88:92:96:98]sts, turn.
Next row: rib 88[92:96:100:102]sts, turn.
Next row: rib 92[96:100:104:106]sts, turn.
Next row: rib 96[100:104:108:110]sts, turn.
Next row: rib 100[104:108:112:114]sts, turn.
Cont in this way, working 4 more sts each end until
152(156:160:168)sts, ending with a **wrong side** row, rib to end.
Buttonhole row: rib 52[52:52:56:56]sts, k2tog, yrn, rib to end.
Change to size 6 (4mm) needles.
Work 2 more rows in rib.
Bind off.

to make up

Sew on sleeves, placing centre of sleeves to shoulder seams. Join side
and sleeve seams. Position and sew button into place.

*" The shaping at the neck creates
an elegant scoop-neck detail
that is flattering to all bust sizes. "*

Look again...

This variation project is the easiest – I simply changed the colour and lengthened the sleeves! This knitted cardigan, inspired by the shape of a bespoke tailored jacket, can be totally transformed by the length of the sleeves. Full-length sleeves give a classic, elegant look, while the rich purple colour is a bold choice.

materials

- 11[11:12:12:13] x 1¾oz (50g) balls of light-weight (DK) bamboo yarn (80% bamboo, 20% extra-fine merino; 116yd/106m per ball) *(photographed in Debbie Bliss Prima, shade 09 Blackcurrant)*
- Pair of size 6 (4mm) needles
- Pair of size 5 (3.75mm) needles
- Stitch holders
- 1 button

Gauge and measurements are as for main garment, apart from sleeve length: 17¾in (45cm) for all sizes

Follow instructions for main garment, until the sleeves:

sleeves

With size 6 (4mm) needles, cast on 62[62:62:72:72]sts.
Starting with a **1st patt row**, work as given for the back, then cont in patt as given for the back until sleeve measures 17¾in (45cm) from cast-on edge, ending with a **wrong side** row.

Then continue with main instructions.

Push the boat out sweater

This classically casual boatneck sweater in ever-chic navy features an allover basketstitch pattern and long sleeves.

" *Here I used a yarn that is 100% silk. Some silk yarns have no elasticity and shed their fibres, but this one has a wonderful drape, and a subtle sheen characteristic of this material.* "

Sweaters don't need to be tight-fitting to be flattering. Sometimes a garment that drapes and flows over the body is more flattering than one that clings to every lump and bump. This is a casual, fairly loose-fitting sweater with a classic boatneck neckline, decorated with pretty buttons on the shoulders.

The basketstich pattern gives the sweater some depth and structure, while the silver trimmings at the edges of the sleeve and round the hem add a touch of chic. Navy and silver is a timeless colour combination that always looks elegant. The silk yarn is wonderfully springy and is beautifully soft to the touch.

Intermediate

measurements

to fit chest	extra small	small	medium	large	extra large
	32–34in	34–36in	36–38in	40–42in	44–46in
	81.5–86.5cm	86.5–91.5cm	91.5–96.5cm	101.5–106.5cm	112–117cm
actual measurement	40¾in	42¾in	45in	48¾in	50¾in
	104cm	109cm	114cm	124cm	129cm
length	22¾in	22¾in	23½in	24½in	25¼in
	58cm	58cm	60cm	62cm	64cm
sleeve length	17¾in	17¾in	17¾in	17¾in	17¾in
	45cm	45cm	45cm	45cm	45cm

materials

- ❀ Yarn **A**: 12(12:12:13:13) x 1¾oz (50g) balls of navy blue silk yarn (100% silk)
- ❀ Yarn **B**: 1 x 1¾oz (50g) ball of silver-coloured silk yarn (100% silk; 137yd/125m per ball)
  *(photographed in (**A**) Louisa Harding Mulberry Silk, shade 13 Navy and (**B**) Louisa Harding Mulberry Silk, shade 2 Silver)*
- ❀ Pair of size 5 (3.75mm) needles
- ❀ Pair of size 3 (3.25mm) needles
- ❀ Stitch holders
- ❀ 8[8:10:10:12] buttons

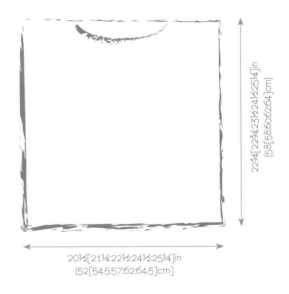

22¾[22¾:23½:24½:25¼]in (58[58:60:62:64]cm)

20½[21¼:22½:24½:25¼]in (52[54.5:57:62:64.5]cm)

gauge

24sts and 38rows to 4in (10cm) square over patt using size 5 (3.75mm) needles and yarn **A**

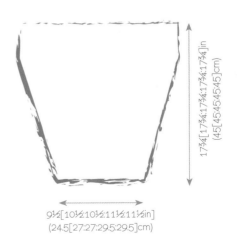

17¾[17¾:17¾:17¾:17¾]in (45[45:45:45:45]cm)

9½[10½:10½:11½:11½in] (24.5[27:27:29.5:29.5]cm)

"On paper the sweater looks like a square box. When it is knitted in the silk yarn, the shape completely transforms into a desirable sweater that shows off your best features."

For another look, the buttonhole bands can be worked in the contrast shade, with the edging also picked up in the contrast. The buttons can then either complement the contrasting colour or match the main shade.

back

With size 5 (3.75mm) needles and yarn **B**, cast on 125[131:137:149:155]sts.

Starting with a **knit** row, st st 3 rows.

Change to yarn **A**.

Knit 5 rows.

1st row (wrong side): k4, [p3, k3] to last st, k1.

2nd row (right side): knit.

Rep the last 2 rows once more.

Knit 4 rows.

9th row (wrong side): p4, [k3, p3] to last st, p1.

10th row (right side): knit.

Rep the last 2 rows once more.

Knit 4 rows.

These 16 rows form the patt.

Rep the last 16 rows until back measures 20½[20½:21¼:22:22¾]in (52[52:54:56:58]cm) from cast-on edge, ending with a **wrong side** row.

Keeping patt correct shape neck as folls:

shape right neck

Next row: patt 43[45:47:51:53]sts, leave rem 82sts on a holder, turn and patt to end.

Dec one st at neck edge of next and every foll row until there are 30[32:34:38:40]sts.

Cont in patt until back measures 22¾[22¾:23½:24½:25¼]in (58[58:60:62:64]cm) from cast-on edge, ending with a **wrong side** row. Knit 3 rows.

Bind off.

The neck edging is worked by picking up stitches round the neckline and knitting a few rows in garter stitch. This creates a neat, firm edge and adds another chic touch to this classic-looking sweater.

shape left neck

With right side of work facing, leave 39[41:43:47:49]sts on a holder, rejoin yarn to rem 43[45:47:51:53]sts.

Work to match right neck reversing shapings.

front

Work as given for the back, until all shaping has been worked and finishing before the instructions 'Knit 3 rows', leaving 30[32:34:38:40]sts on a holder.

With right side facing, rejoin yarn to 30[32:34:38:40]sts of one side. Knit one row.

Buttonhole row: k5[6:4:6:4], [k2tog, yrn, k4]to last 1[2:0:2:0]st, k1[2:0:2:0].

Knit one row.

Bind off.

Work other side to match.

sleeves

With size 5 (3.75mm) needles and yarn **B**, cast on 59[65:65:71:71]sts.

Starting with a **knit** row, st st 3 rows.

Change to yarn **A**.

Knit 5 rows.

Starting with a **1st row**, as given for the back, cont in patt until sleeve measures 4in (10cm) from cast-on edge, ending with a **wrong side** row.

Keeping patt correct, inc one st at each end of next and every foll 6th row until there are 101[107:107:113:113]sts.

Cont without shaping in patt until sleeve measures 17¾in (45cm) from cast-on edge, ending with a **wrong side** row.

Bind off.

The silver edgings are worked in stockinette stitch. The nature of this knitted fabric means that it will automatically roll up on itself, creating a neat-looking rolled edge that shows the wrong side (the purl side) of the fabric.

edging (front and back alike)

With right side facing, yarn **A** and size 3 (3.25mm) needles, pick up and knit 26sts one neck edge, patt 39[41:43:47:49]sts from holder at centre, pick up and knit 26sts along other neck neck. 91[93:95:99:101]sts.

Knit 2 rows.

Bind off.

to make up

Position and sew buttons into place. Slip stitch sleeve edge of buttonhole band on top of buttonband. Sew on sleeves, placing centre of sleeves to centre of buttonbands. Join side and sleeve seams.

"I am fascinated by buttons. I love the fact that by choosing just the right buttons you can make a garment extra special."

Kimono-sleeved smock

This fabulous smock is not for shrinking violets: the punchy colour is the perfect match for the flamboyant shape.

> "This vibrant purple yarn is a blend of three fibres: silk gives the fabric sheen and lustre; wool adds warmth, and mohair brings softness and a haze of longer, fluffy fibres. This creates quite a dense, firm knitted fabric."

This bold-coloured garment shows perfectly that an item does not need to be tight-fitting to be flattering. This smock is designed to have several inches of positive ease, so it will billow and drape rather than clinging. The intricate cable stitch pattern adds detail and interest to the top part of the garment, before falling in elegant folds worked in stockinette stitch.

The full, kimono-style sleeves carry through the smock's extravagant styling. This is a longer-length garment, falling to about hip-length. A gentle scoop neck adds a further chic touch, giving the illusion of a longer neck and flattering the bust.

measurements

to fit chest	extra small 30–32in 76.5–81.5cm	small 34–36in 86.5–91.5cm	medium 36–38in 91.5–96.5cm	large 40–42in 101.5–106.5cm	extra large 44–46in 112–117cm
actual measurement	38¾in 98.5cm	42in 106.5cm	44½in 113.5cm	47½in 121cm	50½in 128.5cm
length	27½in 70cm	27½in 70cm	28¼in 72cm	29¼in 74cm	29¾in 76cm
sleeve length	13¾in 35cm	13¾in 35cm	13¾in 35cm	13¾in 35cm	13¾in 35cm

materials

- ❊ 14[15:16:17:18] x 1½oz (40g) hanks of fine-weight (4ply) silk mohair yarn (35% silk, 30% mohair, 35% wool; 131yd/120m) *(photographed in Noro Maiko, shade 108 Medium Purple)*
- ❊ Pair of size 3 (3.25mm) needles
- ❊ Pair of size 2/3 (3mm) needles
- ❊ Cable needles
- ❊ Stitch holders

gauge

32sts and 32rows to 4in (10cm) square over patt when slightly stretched using size 3 (3.25mm) needles
26sts and 32rows to 4in (10cm) square over st st using size 3 (3.25mm) needles

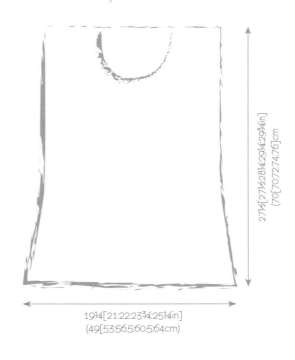

27½[27½:28¼:29¼:29¾in]
(70[70:72:74:76]cm)

19¼[21:22:23¾:25¼in]
(49[53:56.5:60.5:64cm)

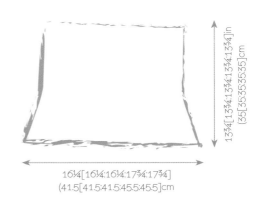

13¾[13¾:13¾:13¾:13¾]in
(35[35:35:35:35]cm)

16¼[16¼:16¼:17¾:17¾]
(41.5[41.5:41.5:45.5:45.5]cm)

> "The smock looks great styled with a poloneck with black jeans. It would look just as good over a T-shirt and shorts to keep warm on summer evenings."

back

With size 3 (3.25mm) needles, cast on 158[170:182:194:206]sts.
Starting with a **knit** row, cont in st st until back measures
12½[12½:13¼:14¼:14¾]in (32[32:34:36:38]cm) from cast-on edge,
ending with a **wrong side** row.
1st patt row (right side): knit to end.
2nd and every alt patt row: purl to end.
3rd patt row: k1, [C4B, k4, C4F]to last st, k1.
5th patt row: as **1st patt row.**
7th patt row: k3, C4FC4B, [k4, C4FC4B]to last 3sts, k3.
These 8 rows form the cable patt.
Rep the last 8 rows until back measures 27½[27½:28¼:29¼:29¾]in
(70[70:72:74:76]cm) from cast-on edge, ending with a **wrong
side** row.

shape shoulders

Bind off 44[48:52:56:60]sts at the beg of the next 2 rows.
Leave centre 70[74:78:82:86]sts on a holder.

front

Work as given for the back until front measures
22[22:22¾:23½:24½]in (56[56:58:60:62]cm) from cast-on edge,
ending with a **wrong side** row.

*The patterned section at the top of the garment is designed
to fall a few inches under your bust. If you want to create
more of an empire-line effect and more of an hourglass shape,
you could start the stockinette section of the body so it falls
directly under the bust.*

shape left neck

Next row: patt 52[56:60:64:68]sts, turn, slip rem sts on a holder.
Keeping patt correct, dec one st at neck edge of next and every foll
row until there are 44[48:52:56:60]sts.
Cont without shaping in cable patt, until front measures
27½[27½:28¼:29¼:29¾]in (70[70:72:74:76]cm) from cast-on edge,
ending with a **wrong side** row.
Bind off.

shape right neck

With right side facing, leave centre 54[58:62:66:70]sts on a holder,
rejoin yarn to rem 52[56:60:64:68]sts, patt to end.
Work to match left neck, reversing shapings.

sleeves

With size 3 (3.25mm) needles, cast on 134[134:134:146:146]sts.
Starting with a **knit** row, cont in st st until sleeve measures 6in (15cm)
from cast-on edge, ending with a **wrong side** row.
Starting with a **1st patt row** as given for the back, cont in cable patt
until sleeve measures 13¾in (35cm) from cast-on edge, ending with a
wrong side row.
Bind off.

*The full, billowing sleeves perfectly complement the flowing,
swingy shape of the body of the sweater.*

neck edge

Join right shoulder seam. With right side facing and size 2/3
(3mm) needles, pick up and knit 36sts down left front neck, knit
54[58:62:66:70]sts from holder at centre front, pick up and knit 36sts
up right front neck, knit 70[74:78:82:86]sts from holder at centre
back. 196[204:212:220:228]sts.
Next row: k0[4:1:5:2], [k5, k2tog] over centre back sts,
k41[38:42:39:36], [k5, k2tog]over centre front sts, knit to end.
179[186:193:200:206]sts.
Knit one row.
Bind off.

to make up

Join left shoulder and neckband seam. Sew on sleeves, placing centre
of sleeves to shoulder seams. Join side and sleeve seams.

*The neckline is finished with a narrow band of garter stitch
to create a neat edge. The gentle scoop shape of the neckline
will make a flattering frame for your face and neck.*

“ *The cable pattern is easy to follow – it is only a 4-row repeat, yet the result looks very intricate.* ”

Twice as nice cardigan

This simple design uses two different rib patterns to give an elegant figure-skimming fit.

This no-fuss knit guarantees figure-flattering results. The main body is knitted with no shaping; a change of stitch pattern and the body-hugging ribbed fabric creates all the shape you need. Ribbing over the chest adds definition to smaller busts, but won't distort a larger one. The button fastening allows the fabric to fall away from the body under the bust, skimming over the hips with no unflattering stretch.

You could throw this cardigan over a T-shirt or a dress on a cool summer evening. Come colder days, the close-fitting sleeves and longer length will add warmth when layered with a scarf and thick gloves. The streamlined shape of the garment gives balance to all figure types.

" The variegated effect of the hand-dyed yarn adds fantastic visual movement and depth of colour to the simple silhouette."

measurements

to fit chest	extra small	small	medium	large	extra large
	30-32in	34-36in	36-38in	40-42in	44-46in
	76.5-81.5cm	86.5-91.5cm	91.5-96.5cm	101.5-106.5cm	112-117cm
actual measurement	33in	37¾ in	39¼in	43½in	47¾in
	84cm	96cm	100cm	110.5cm	121.5cm
length	25¼in	25¼in	26in	26¾in	27½in
	64cm	64cm	66cm	68cm	70cm
sleeve length	17¾in	17¾in	17¾in	17¾in	17¾in
	45cm	45cm	45cm	45cm	45cm

materials

* 9[10:10:11:11] x 1¾oz (50g) hanks of medium-weight (DK) wool (hand-dyed 100% merino wool; 137yd/125m per hank) *(photographed in Mirasol Hacho, shade 311 Cinnamon Roll)*
* Pair of size 6 (4mm) needles
* Pair of size 5 (3.75mm) needles
* Stitch holders
* 3 buttons

gauge

22sts and 30 rows to 4in (10cm) square over rib patt when stretched using size 6 (4mm) needles

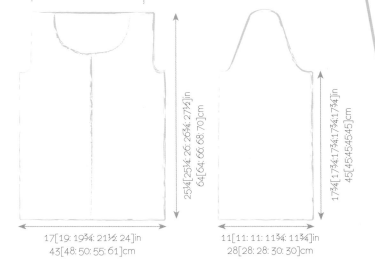

25¼[25¼: 26: 26¾: 27½]in
64[64: 66: 68: 70]cm

17[19: 19¾: 21½: 24]in
43[48: 50: 55: 61]cm

17¾[17¾:17¾:17¾:17¾]in
45[45:45:45:45]cm

11[11: 11: 11¾: 11¾]in
28[28: 28: 30: 30]cm

back

With size 6 (4mm) needles, cast on 94[106:110:122:134]sts.
1st patt row: knit to end.
2nd patt row: p2, [k2, p2]to end.
These 2 rows form the g st rib patt.
Rep the last 2 rows until back measures 11¾in (30cm) from cast-on edge, ending with a **wrong side** row.
1st rib row (right side): k2, [p2, k2]to end.
2nd rib row: p2, [k2, p2]to end.
These 2 rows form the rib patt.
Rep the last 2 rows until the back measures 16½[16½:17½:17½:18]in (42[42:44:44:46]cm from cast-on edge, ending with a **wrong side** row.

The change of stitch pattern from garter stitch rib to 2x2 rib means that the cardigan is close-fitting round the chest but more free-flowing from under the bust to the hips, creating a flattering body-skimming line.

" The vertical lines of the rib stitches elongate the torso to create a slimming effect."

shape armholes

Bind off 5sts at the beg of the next 2 rows. 84[96:100:112:124]sts.
Dec one st at each end of next and 4 foll 4th rows.
74[86:90:102:114]sts.
Cont without shaping in rib patt until armhole measures 8¾[8¾:8¾:9½:9½]in (22[22:22:24:24]cm from start of armhole shaping, ending with a wrong side row.

Bind off 19[24:26:30:36]sts at the beg of the next 2 rows.
Leave centre 36[38:38:42:42] sts on a holder.

left front

With size 6 (4mm) needles, cast on 47[51:55:59:67]sts.

1st patt row: knit to end.

2nd patt row: p3, [k2, p2]to end.

These 2 rows form the g st rib patt.

Rep the last 2 rows until left front measures 11¾in (30cm) from cast-on edge, ending with a **wrong side** row.

1st rib row (right side): [k2, p2]to last 3sts, k3.

2nd rib row: p3, [k2, p2]to end.

These 2 rows form the rib patt.

Rep the last 2 rows until the left front measures 16½[16½:17½:17½:18]in (42[42:44:44:46]cm) from cast-on edge, ending with a **wrong side** row.

The neckline is finished off with a narrow edging in garter stitch. The combination of the scoop neck and delicate trim will elongate your neck for an elegant look.

Bind off 5sts at the beg of the next row. 42[46:50:54:62]sts.

Work one row.

Dec one st at armhole edge of next row and 4 foll 4th rows, ending with a right side row. 37[41:45:49:57]sts.

Next row: rib 14[14:14:15:16]sts, slip these sts on a holder, rib to end.

Dec one st at the neck edge of next and every foll alt row until 19[24:26:30:36]sts rem.

Cont without shaping in rib patt until armhole measures 8¾[8¾:8¾:9½:9½]in (22[22:22:24:24]cm) from start of armhole shaping, ending with a **wrong side** row.

Bind off.

right front

With size 6 (4mm) needles, cast on 47[51:55:59:67]sts.

1st patt row: knit to end.

2nd patt row: [p2, k2]to last 3sts, p3.

These 2 rows form the g st rib patt.

Rep the last 2 rows until right front measures 11¾in (30cm) from cast-on edge, ending with a **wrong side** row.

1st rib row (right side): k3, [p2, k2]to end.

2nd rib row: [p2, k2]to last 3sts, p3.

These 2 rows form the rib patt.

Rep the last 2 rows until the right front measures 16½[16½:17½:17½:18]in (42[42:44:44:46]cm) from cast-on edge, ending with a **right side** row.

Work to match left front, reversing shapings.

sleeves

With size 6 (4mm) needles, cast on 62[62:62:66:66]sts.

Starting with a **1st patt row** as given for the back, cont in g st rib patt until sleeve measures 9¾in (25cm) from cast-on edge, ending with a **wrong side** row.

Starting with a **1st rib row** as given for the back, cont in rib patt until sleeve measures 17¾in (45cm) from cast-on edge, ending with a **wrong side** row.

Bind off 5sts at the beg of the next 2 rows. 52[52:52:56:56]sts.

Dec one st at each end of next and 6 foll 4th rows. 38[38:38:42:42]sts.

Work one row.

Dec one st at each end of next and 4 foll alt rows. 28[28:28:32:32]sts.

Work one row.

Dec one st at each end of next and every foll row until 14[14:14:16:16]sts rem.

Bind off 5sts at the beg of the next 2 rows. 4[4:4:6:6]sts.

Bind off rem sts.

buttonband left edging

With right side facing and size 5 (3.75mm) needles, pick up and knit 105sts down left front opening edge.

Knit 2 rows.

Bind off.

buttonhole right edging

With right side facing and size 5 (3.75mm) needles, pick up and knit 105sts up right front opening edge.

Knit one row.

Buttonhole row: knit to last 24sts, [k2tog, yrn, k7]twice, k2tog, yrn, k4.

Bind off.

neck edging

Join shoulder seams. With right side facing and size 5 (3.75mm) needles, pick up and knit one st from edging, knit 14[14:14:15:16]sts from holder at right front, pick up and knit 37[37:37:41:41]sts up right front neck, knit 36[38:38:42:42]sts from holder at centre back, pick up and knit 37[37:37:41:41]sts down left front neck, knit 14[14:14:15:16]sts from holder at left front, pick up and knit one st from edging. 140[142:142:156:158]sts.

Knit 2 rows.

Bind off.

to make up

Sew on sleeves, placing centre of sleeves to shoulder seams. Join side and sleeve seams. Position and sew buttons into place.

“ *The shaping at the neck creates an elegant scoop-neck detail that is flattering to all bust sizes.* ”

Look again...

This striking variation shows just how different the garment can look when knitted in an alternative colourway, this time a vibrant palette of pinks and purples. The effect is funky and fashionable; you could dress it up or down with daywear or nightwear for fabulous results. The ribbed pattern creates a wonderfully shapely and streamlined silhouette without clinging to every lump and bump.

materials

- ✳ 9[10:10:11:11] x 1¾oz (50g) hanks of medium-weight (DK) wool (hand-dyed 100% merino wool; 137yd/125m per hank) *(photographed in Mirasol Hacho, shade 309 Double Fuchsia)*
- ✳ Pair of size 6 (4mm) needles
- ✳ Pair of size 5 (3.75mm) needles
- ✳ Stitch holders
- ✳ 3 buttons

Gauge and measurements are as for main garment.

" *The beauty of an all-over ribbed pattern in a pure wool yarn is that the knitted fabric stretches smoothly and evenly to fit your every curve.* "

Cosy cables

This wonderfully cuddly jumper features fabulous vertical cable bands set against a background of reverse stockinette stitch.

Cables are great fun to knit – they're not nearly as complicated as you might expect, but the beautifully intricate patterns look very impressive! The vertical lines of the cable bands and longer length of the sweater, reaching to the hip, creates a flatteringly long and lean outline. Stretchy ribbing creates a neat edge to the hem and cuffs, as well as making the cosy poloneck.

This is just the thing to reach for on a winter's day; lighter and less restricting than a heavy winter coat, it will keep you just as warm and add much-needed colour when the weather is cold and grey. The deep poloneck means you won't even need to wear a scarf!

" *This gorgeous yarn is a lush blend of merino wool, silk and alpaca, combining warmth with a beautiful sheen and softness.* "

measurements

to fit chest	extra small	small	medium	large	extra large
	32–34in	36–38in	40–42in	44–46in	48–50in
	81.5–86.5cm	91.5–96.5cm	101.5–106.5cm	111.5–117cm	122–127cm
actual measurement	36½in	40¼in	44¼in	48¼in	52¼in
	92.5cm	102.5cm	112.5cm	122.5cm	132.5cm
length	25¼in	25¼in	26in	26¾in	27½in
	64cm	64cm	66cm	68cm	70cm
sleeve length	17¾in	17¾in	17¾in	17¾in	17¾in
	45cm	45cm	45cm	45cm	45cm

materials

- 23[24:25:26] x 1¾oz (50g) hanks of bulky-weight (chunky) alpaca silk yarn (60% merino wool, 20% alpaca, 20% silk; 55yd/50m per hank) *(photographed in Mirasol Sulka, shade 215 Raspberry)*
- Pair of size 10 (6mm) needles
- Cable needle
- Stitch holders

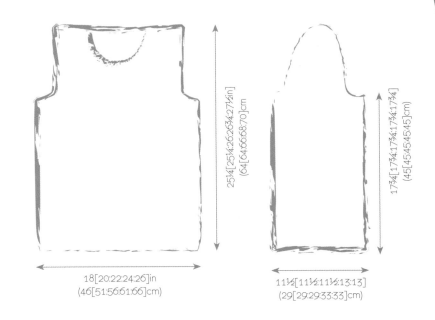

25¼[25¼:26:26¾:27½in] (64[64:66:68:70]cm)

18[20:22:24:26]in (46[51:56:61:66]cm)

17¾[17¾:17¾:17¾:17¾] (45[45:45:45:45]cm)

11½[11½:11½:13:13] (29[29:29:33:33]cm)

gauge

20sts and 21rows to 4in (10cm) square over patt when stretched using size 10 (6mm) needles

Cables look so beautiful but can sometimes be complicated. This cable pattern is a simple 4-row repeat with only two simple cable instructions: C4B and C4F.

"*The yarn used here is beautiful to knit with, and because it's chunky you can see the cables grow quickly.*"

back

With size 10 (6mm) needles, cast on 68[76:84:92:100]sts.

1st rib row: p3, [k2, p2]to last st, p1.

2nd rib row: k3, [p2, k2]to last st, k1.

These 2 rows form the rib patt.

Rep the last 2 rows until rib measures 2in (5cm) from cast-on edge, ending with a **right side** row.

Inc row (wrong side): k3, p2, k2, p2[6:10:14:18], *k2, p2, m1, k2, m1, p2, m1, k2, m1, rep from * to last 9[13:17:21:25]sts, p2[6:10:14:18], k2, p2, k3. 88[96:104:112:120]sts.

1st patt row (right side): p3, k2, p2, k2[6:10:14:18]] *p2, k2, [C4F]twice, p2, rep from * to last 9[13:17:21:25]sts, k2[6:10:14:18], p2, k2, p3.

2nd and 4th patt row (wrong side): k3, p2, k2, p2[6:10:14:18], *k2, p10, k2, rep from * to last 9[13:17:21:25]sts, p2[6:10:14:18], k2, p2, k3.

3rd patt row: p3, k2, p2, k2[6:10:14:18], *p2, [C4B]twice, k2, p2, rep from * to last 9[13:17:21:25]sts, p2[6:10:14:18], k2, p2, k3.

These 4 rows form the patt.

Rep the last 4 rows until the back measures 16½[16½:17½:17½:18]in (42[42:44:44:46]cm) from cast-on edge, ending with a **wrong side** row.

shape armholes

Bind off 4sts at the beg of the next 2 rows. 80[88:96:104:112]sts.

Dec one st at each each of next and 4 foll alt rows. 70[78:86:94:102]sts.

Keeping patt correct, cont without shaping until armhole measures 8½[8½:8½:9½:9½]in (22[22:22:24:24]cm) from start of armhole shaping, ending with a **wrong side** row.

shape shoulders

Bind off 15[18:21:24:27]sts at the beg of the next 2 rows.

Leave centre 40[42:44:46:48]sts on a holder.

front

Work as given for the back until armhole measures 5½[5½:5½:6¼:6¼]in (14[14:14:16:16]cm) from start of armhole shaping, ending with a **wrong side** row.

shape left neck

Next row: Patt 26[29:32:35:38]sts, slip rem sts on a holder, turn, patt to end.

Keeping patt correct, dec one st at the neck edge of next and every foll row until there are 15[18:21:24:27]sts.

Cont without shaping in the patt until armhole measures 8½[8½:8½:9½:9½]in (22[22:22:24:24]cm) from start of armhole shaping, ending with a **wrong side** row.

Bind off.

shape right neck

With right side facing, leave centre 18[20:22:24:26]sts on a holder, rejoin yarn to rem 26[29:32:35:38]sts, patt to end.

Work to match left neck, reversing shapings.

sleeves

With size 10 (6mm) needles, cast on 42[42:42:50:50]sts.

1st rib row: p2, [k2, p2]to end.

2nd rib row: k2, [p2, k2]to end.

These 2 rows form the rib patt.

Rep the last 2 rows until rib measures 2in (5cm) from cast-on edge, ending with a **right side** row.

Inc 16sts evenly along the next row. 58[58:58:66:66]sts.

1st patt row (right side): p1[1:1:5:5], *p2, k2, [C4F]twice, p2 rep from * to last 1[1:1:5:5]st(s), purl to end.

2nd and 4th patt row (wrong side): k1[1:1:5:5], *k2, p10, k2, rep from * to last 1[1:1:5:5]st(s), knit to end.

3rd patt row: p1[1:1:5:5], *p2, [C4B]twice, k2, p2, rep from * to last 1[1:1:5:5]st(s), purl to end.

Cont in patt until sleeve measures 17¾in (45cm) from cast-on edge, ending with a **wrong side** row.

The ribbed cuffs on the sleeves make a stylish counterpoint to the ribbing at the bottom edge and the ribbed poloneck.

Shape top

Bind off 4sts at the beg of the next 2 rows. 50[50:50:58:58]sts.

Dec one st at each end of next and 4 foll 4th rows. 40[40:40:48:48]sts.

Work one row.

Dec one st at each end of next and 6 foll alt rows. 26[26:26:34:34]sts.

Work one row.

Bind off.

neck

Join right shoulder seam. With right side facing and size 10 (6mm) needles, pick up and knit 12sts down left front neck, knit 18[20:22:24:26]sts from holder at centre front, pick up and knit 12sts up right front neck, knit 40[42:44:46:48]sts at centre back. 82[86:90:94:98]sts.

1st rib row: p2, [k2, p2]to end.

2nd rib row: k2, [p2, k2]to end.

Rep the last 2 rows until neck measures 6in (15cm), ending with a wrong side row.

Bind off.

to make up

Join left shoulder seam and collar edge. Sew on sleeves, placing centre of sleeves to shoulder seams. Join side and sleeve seams.

Huggable hoodie

This cuddly, close-fitting hooded sweater is a timeless item that will get you through a cold winter in style.

When the temperature drops it's easy to forget about looking stylish for the sake of keeping warm. This sweater offers an alternative: it's huggably warm and cosy but also well-fitted and flattering to a wide variety of body shapes. The addition of the hood adds a funky, casual element as well as being practical.

The allover honeycomb cable stitch is miraculously stretchy and forgiving, fitting snugly to your curves without looking bulky and adding pounds where you don't want them.

"This cosy sweater is made in classic merino yarn, which makes a firm, sturdy and warm fabric. I chose a solid shade in a warm chestnut brown."

measurements

to fit chest	extra small	small	medium	large	extra large
	32–34in	36–38in	38–40in	40–44in	46–48in
	81.5–86.5cm	91.5–96.5cm	96.5–101.5cm	101.5–112cm	117–122cm
actual measurement	39¼in	44in	49in	53¾in	58½in
	100cm	112cm	124.5cm	136.5cm	149cm
length	23½in	24½in	25¼in	25¼in	26in
	60cm	62cm	64cm	64cm	66cm
sleeve length	17¾in	17¾in	17¾in	17¾in	17¾in
	45cm	45cm	45cm	45cm	45cm

materials

- 9[10:10:11:11] x 3½oz (100g) hanks of light-weight (DK) kettle-dyed wool yarn (100% merino; 216yd/197m per hank) *(photographed in Malabrigo Worsted, shade 512 Chestnut)*
- Pair of size 8 (5mm) needles
- Pair of size 6 (4mm) needles
- Cable needle
- Stitch holders
- 6 buttons

gauge

26sts and 30 rows to 4in (10cm) square over patt when stretched using size 8 (5mm) needles

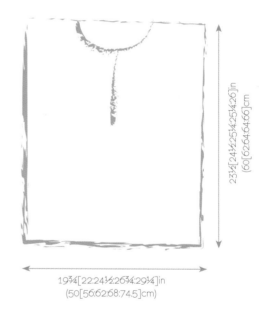

23½[24½:25¼:25¼:26]in
(60[62:64:64:66]cm)

19¾[22:24½:26¾:29¼]in
(50[56:62:68:74.5]cm)

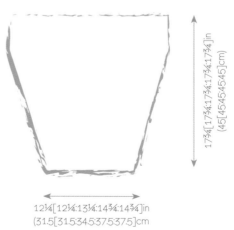

17¾[17¾:17¾:17¾:17¾]in
(45[45:45:45:45]cm)

12¼[12¼:13¼:14¾:14¾]in
(31.5[31.5:34.5:37.5:37.5]cm)

"I hope this hoodie becomes an old favourite, comfortable and easy to wear yet still flattering."

back

With size 8 (5mm) needles, cast on 130[146:162:178:194]sts.

1st rib row: k2, [p2, k2]to end.

2nd rib row: p2, [k2, p2]to end.

These 2 rows form the rib patt.

Rep the last 2 rows once more.

1st patt row (right side): knit to end.

2nd patt row: purl to end.

3rd patt row: k1, [C4B, C4F]to last st, k1.

4th patt row: as 2nd patt row.

5th patt row: as 1st patt row.

6th patt row: as 2nd patt row.

7th patt row: k1, [C4FC4B]to last st, k1.

8th patt row: as 2nd patt row.

These 8 rows form the patt.

Rep the last 8 rows until back measures 23½[24½:25¼:25¼:26]in (60[62:64:64:66]cm) from cast-on edge, ending with a **wrong side** row.

shape shoulders

Bind off 38[42:48:54:58]sts at the beg of the next 2 rows.
Leave centre 54[62:66:70:78]sts on a holder.

front

Work as given for the back until front measures 13¼[14¼:14¾:14¾:15¾]in (34[36:38:38:40]cm) from cast-on edge, ending with **wrong side** row.

shape left side

Next row: Patt until there are 65[73:81:89:97]sts on the right-hand needle, slip rem sts on a holder, turn.

Next row: Inc one st at neck edge. 66[74:82:90:98]sts.

Cont without shaping in patt with edge sts as k1 until front measures 21¼[22:22¾:22¾:23½]in (54[56:58:58:60]cm) from cast-on edge, ending with a **right side** row.

shape left neck

Next row: Patt 15[19:21:23:27]sts, slip these sts on a holder, patt to end.

Work one row.

Dec one st at neck edge of the next and every foll row until 38[42:48:54:58]sts rem.

Cont without shaping in patt, until front measures 23½[24½:25¼:25¼:26]in (60[62:64:64:66]cm) from cast-on edge, ending with a **wrong side** row.

Bind off.

shape right side and neck

With right side facing, rejoin yarn to rem sts, patt to end.

Work to match left side and neck, reversing shapings.

sleeves

With size 8 (5mm) needles, cast on 82[82:90:98:98]sts.

Starting with a **1st rib row** as given for the back, work 4 rows in rib.

Starting with a **1st patt row** as given for the back, cont in patt until sleeve measures 2¾in (7cm) from cast on edge, ending with a **wrong side** row.

Keeping patt correct, inc one st at each end of next and every foll 4th row until there are 102[106:114:114:122]sts.

Cont without shaping in patt until sleeve measures 17¾in (45cm) from cast-on edge, ending with a **wrong side** row.

Bind off.

The sleeves and the bottom of the garment are edged in ribbing for a neat finish. This style element is repeated on the edging of the hood.

hood

Join shoulder seams. With right side facing and size 6 (4mm) needles, k15[19:21:23:27]sts from holder at right front, pick up and knit 15sts up right front neck, k54[62:66:70:78]sts from holder at centre back, pick up and knit 15sts down left front neck, k15[19:21:23:27]sts from holder at left front. 114[130:138:146:162]sts.

Purl one row.

Change to size 8 (5mm) needles.

Starting with a **1st patt row** as given for the back, cont in patt until hood measures 13¼in (34cm), ending with a **wrong side** row.

Bind off.

edging

Join bound-off edges of hood. With right side facing and size 6 (4mm) needles, pick up and knit 50sts up right front opening edge, pick up and knit 158sts around hood, pick up and knit 50sts down left front opening edge. 258sts.

1st rib row (wrong side): p2, [k2, p2]to end.

2nd rib row: k2, [p2, k2]to end.

Work the **1st rib row** once more.

Buttonhole row (right side): [k2, p2, k2tog, yrn, p2]6 times, rib to end.

Work one row in rib.

Bind off.

to make up

Sew on sleeves, placing centre of sleeves to shoulder seams. Join side and sleeve seams. Slip stitch edging ends into place with right edging over left edging. Position and sew buttons into place.

Great lengths coat

This stylish mid-length coat makes a great statement with its rich autumnal hues.

This elegant empire-line coat is knitted in a chunky yarn. Ribbing is used to fit closely around the upper body and the sleeves, while the lower body is made in stockinette stitch to skim the hips. The coat buttons up to just under the bust and then flares elegantly outwards.

This coat will give you a dash of style while hugging you with warmth. Wear it buttoned up in place of a winter coat or leave it open and wear it as a long-line cardigan over some colourful layers. The button-up neck is also versatile; wear it as a poloneck or turn it down into a fold-over collar.

" This chunky variegated yarn creates some wonderful effects as the deep earthy colours merge and tone into one another. "

measurements

to fit chest	extra small 32-34in 81.5-86.5cm	small 34-36in 86.5-91.5cm	medium 36-38in 91.5-96.5cm	large 40-42in 101.5-106.5cm	extra large 44-46in 112-117cm
actual measurement	35¼in 90cm	38in 96.5cm	40½in 103cm	45¾in 116.5cm	51in 130cm
length	30¾in 78cm	30¾in 78cm	31½in 80cm	32¼in 82cm	33in 84cm
sleeve length	17¾in 45cm	17¾in 45cm	17¾in 45cm	17¾in 45cm	17¾in 45cm

materials

- 7[7:8:8:9] x 3½oz (100g) hanks of chunky-weight (bulky) wool silk yarn (75% wool, 25% silk; 131yd/ 120m per hank)
  (photographed in Noro Iro, shade 67 greens, rusts, blue brown)
- Pair of size 10.5 (7mm) needles
- Pair of size 10 (6mm) needles
- Stitch holders
- 6[6:6:7:7] buttons

gauge

12sts and 18 rows to 4in (10cm) square over st st using size 10.5 (7mm) needles

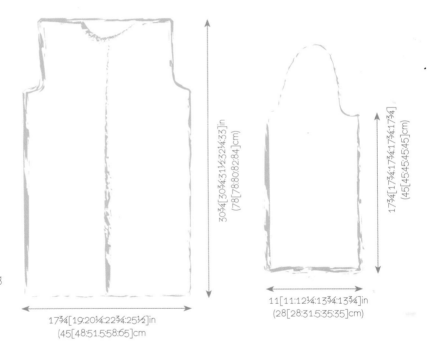

30¾[30¾:31½:32¼:33]in (78[78:80:82:84]cm)

17¾[17¾:17¾:17¾:17¾]in (45[45:45:45:45]cm)

17¾[19:20¼:22¾:25½]in (45[48:51.5:58:65]cm)

11[11:12¼:13¾:13¾]in (28[28:31.5:35:35]cm)

back

With size 10.5 (7mm) needles, cast on 54[58:62:70:78]sts.
Knit 3 rows.
Starting with a **knit** row, cont in st st until back measures 16½in (42cm) from cast-on edge, ending with a **wrong side** row.
1ˢᵗ patt row (right side): k2, [p2, k2]to end.
2ⁿᵈ patt row: p2, [k2, p2]to end.
These 2 rows form the rib patt.
Rep the last 2 rows until the back measures 22[22:22¾:22¾:23½] in (56[56:58:58:60]cm) from cast-on edge, ending with a **wrong side** row.

shape armholes

Bind off 3sts at the beg of the next 2 rows. 48[52:56:64:72]sts.
Dec one st at each end of next and 2 foll 4ᵗʰ rows. 42[46:50:58:66]sts.
Cont without shaping in rib patt until armhole measures 8½[8½:8½:9½:9½]in (22[22:22:24:24]cm) from start of armhole shaping, ending with a **wrong side** row.

shape shoulders

Bind off 11[12:13:16:19]sts at the beg of the next 2 rows.
Leave centre 20[22:24:26:28]sts on a holder.

left front

With size 10.5 (7mm) needles, cast on 29[31:33:37:41]sts.
Knit 3 rows.
1st row: knit
2nd row: k3[5:3:3:3], purl to end.
These 2 rows set the st st with edge 3[5:3:3:3]sts as g st.
Rep the last 2 rows until left front measures 16½in (42cm) from cast-on edge, ending with a **wrong side** row.
1st patt row (right side): [k2, p2]to last 5[7:5:5:5]sts, knit to end.
2nd patt row: k3[5:3:3:3], [p2, k2]to last 2sts, p2.
These 2 rows form the rib patt with edge 3[5:3:3:3]sts as g st.
Rep the last 2 rows until the left front measures 22[22:22¾:22¾:23½]in (56[56:58:58:60]cm) from cast-on edge, ending with a **wrong side** row.

shape armhole

Bind off 3sts at the beg of the next row. 26[28:30:34:38]sts.
Dec one st at armhole edge of next and 2 foll 4th rows. 23[25:27:31:35]sts.
Cont without shaping in rib patt until armhole measures 7[7:7:8:8]in (18[18:18:20:20]cm) from start of armhole shaping, ending with a **right side** row.

shape neck

Next row: patt 8[9:10:11:12]sts, slip these sts on a holder, patt to end.
Dec one st at the neck edge of next and every foll row until there are 11[12:13:16:19]sts.
Cont without shaping in rib patt until armhole measures 8½[8½:8½:9½:9½]in (22[22:22:24:24]cm) from start of armhole shaping, ending with a **wrong side** row.
Bind off.
Mark positions for 4[4:4:5:5] buttons, first one 17¾in (45cm) from cast-on edge, last one ¾in (2cm) from start of neck shaping and remaining 2[2:2:3:3] buttons placed evenly between.

The ribbed section at the top gives a good fit and neat shape to the coat over the bust. The sleeves are also ribbed to be close-fitting and warm.

right front

With size 10.5 (7mm) needles, cast on 29[31:33:37:41]sts.
Knit 3 rows.
1st row: knit
2nd row: purl to last 3[5:3:3:3]sts, knit to end.
These 2 rows set the st st with edge 3[5:3:3:3]sts as g st.
Rep the last 2 rows until right front measures 16½in (42cm) from cast-on edge, ending with a wrong side row.

1st patt row (right side): k5[7:5:5:5], [p2, k2]to end.
2nd patt row: p2, [k2, p2]to last 3[5:3:3:3]sts, knit to end.
These 2 rows form the rib patt with edge 3[5:3:3:3]sts as g st.
Work to match left front, working buttonholes as folls as each button marker is reached:
Buttonhole row (right side): k1, yrn, k2tog, patt to end.

Choose your buttons carefully to increase the style impact of the coat. I went for funky square buttons with a ridged texture, picking up the green tones in the coat.

sleeves

With size 10.5 (7mm) needles, cast on 34[34:38:42:42]sts.
Starting with a **1st patt row** as given for the back, cont in rib patt until sleeve measures 17¾in (45cm) from cast-on edge, ending with a wrong side row.

shape top

Bind off 3sts at the beg of the next 2 rows. 28[28:32:34:34]sts. Dec one st at each end of next and 4 foll 4th rows. 18[18:22:24:24]sts.
Work one row.
Dec one st at each end of next and 2 foll alt rows. 12[12:16:18:18]sts.
Work one row.
Dec one st at each end of next and every foll row until 8[8:12:12:12]sts rem.
Bind off 4[4:6:6:6]sts at the beg of the next 2 rows.

collar

Join shoulder seams. With right side facing and size 10 (6mm) needles, patt 8[9:10:11:12]sts from holder at right front, pick up and knit 6sts up right front neck, k20[22:24:26:28]sts from holder at centre back, pick up and knit 6sts along left front neck, k8[9:10:11:12]sts from holder at left front. 48[52:56:60:64]sts.
1st patt row: k3[5:3:3:3], p2, [k2, p2]to last 3[5:3:3:3]sts, knit to end.
2nd patt row: k5[7:5:5:5], p2, [k2, p2] to last 5[7:5:5:5]sts, knit to end.
Rep the last 2 rows until collar measures 1½in (4cm), ending with a **wrong side** row.
Work a **buttonhole row** as given for the right front.
Cont in rib patt until collar measures 4in (10cm), ending with a **wrong side** row.
Work a **buttonhole row** as given for the right front.
Cont in rib patt until collar measures 4¾in (12cm), ending with a **wrong side** row.
Bind off.

to make up

Sew on sleeves, placing centre of sleeves to shoulder seams. Join side and sleeve seams. Position and sew buttons into place.

Look again...

This variation features simple but striking modifications: I shortened the sleeves and lengthened the collar. These small changes result in dramatic differences, particularly when the coat is knitted in a solid pastel colour. The shorter sleeves create a chic and unexpected look when worked in a chunky yarn. The over-size fold-down collar is a lovely warm feature that will keep you cosy and stylish through the colder months.

> *" The solid colour yarn accentuates the flattering shape of the coat. The yarn has a small amount of cashmere mixed in with wool for a touch of luxury. "*

materials

- 21[22:24:25] x 1¾oz (50g) balls of chunky-weight (bulky) wool and cashmere blend (90% wool, 10% cashmere; 46yd/42m per ball) *(photographed in Debbie Bliss Como, shade 07 denim blue)*
- Pair of size 10.5 (7mm) needles
- Pair of size 10 (6mm) needles
- Stitch holders
- 6[6:6:7:7] buttons

Gauge and measurements are as for main garment, apart from sleeve length: 11¾in (30cm) for all sizes

Follow instructions for main garment, until the sleeves:

sleeves

With size 10.5 (7mm) needles, cast on 34[34:38:42:42]sts.
Starting with a **1st patt row** as given for the back, cont in rib patt until sleeve measures 11¾in (30cm) from cast-on edge, ending with a **wrong side** row.

Then continue with main instructions, until the collar:

collar

Join shoulder seams. With right side facing and size 10 (6mm) needles, k8[9:10:11:12]sts from holder at right front, pick up and knit 6sts up right front neck, k20[22:24:26:28]sts from holder at centre back, pick up and knit 6sts along left front neck, k8[9:10:11:12]sts from holder at left front. 48[52:56:60:64]sts

1st patt row: k3[5:3:3:3], p2, [k2, p2]to last 3[5:3:3:3]sts, knit to end.
2nd patt row: k5[7:5:5:5], p2, [k2, p2] to last 5[7:5:5:5]sts, knit to end.
Rep the last 2 rows until collar measures 1½in (4cm), ending with a **wrong side** row.
Work a **buttonhole row** as given for the right front.
Cont in rib patt until collar measures 4in (10cm), ending with a **wrong side** row.
Work another **buttonhole row.**
Cont in rib patt until collar measures 4¾in (12cm), ending with a **wrong side** row.
Change to size 10.5 (7mm) needles. Cont in patt until collar measures 7¾in (20cm), ending with a **wrong side** row.
Bind off.

Make up as for main instructions.

Techniques

In this section I outline the main
techniques that you will need to knit the
garments featured in this book. I haven't
included the most basic techniques
such as casting on, making the knit and
purl stitches, and binding off. Instead
I've focused on describing the methods
that you will need to achieve a great fit
and professional-looking finish to your
garment. If you do need a reminder of
the basics, or are just learning to knit,
there are lots of great reference books
available, including Claire Crompton's
The Knitter's Bible (David & Charles).

Abbreviations

Knitting patterns tend to use a lot of abbreviations to save on space and avoid the repetition of frequently used terms. These can look a bit bewildering on first glance, but you will soon become familiar with this knitting language. Below are listed all the terms that are used in the knitting patterns in this book.

alt	alternate	C4B	slip next 2sts onto cable needle and leave at back of work, k2, then k2 from cable needle	k2togtbl	knit two stitches together through the back loop (decrease by one stitch)	st st	stockinette stitch (stocking stitch) [knit 1 row, purl 1 row]
beg	beginning					st(s)	stitch(es)
C2B	cable two back; miss the first stitch on the left-hand needle and knit into the front of the second stitch. Do not slip the worked stitch off the needle, but knit into the front of the first stitch (the 'missed stitch'). Slip both the stitches off the needle together.	C4F	slip next 2sts onto cable needle and leave at front of work, k2, then k2 from cable needle	m1	make one (increase by one stitch)	rev st st	reverse stockinette stitch (purl side is the 'right' side)
		cm	centimetre(s)	p	purl	ybk	yarn back
		cont	continue	p2tog	purl two stitches together (decrease by one stitch)	yrn	yarn round needle or yarn over needle
		dec	decrease				
C2F	knit the second stitch on the left-hand needle through the back, working behind the first stitch. Then knit into the front of the first stitch. Slip both the stitches off the needle together.	foll	following	p3tog	purl three stitches together		
		g st	garter stitch [knit every row]	patt	pattern		
		in	inch(es)	psso	pass the slipped stitch over		
		inc	increase	rem	remaining		
		k	knit	rep	repeat		
		k2 tog	knit two stitches together (decrease by one stitch)	RHN	right-hand needle		
				s1	slip one stitch		

Shaping

Most of my designs do not feature waist shaping; instead the garments are close-fitting due to the stitch pattern used, such as ribbing or other stretchy knitted fabrics. However, you will need to use increases and decreases in other areas, such as shaping a sleeve or a neckline. You will also need to combine increases and decreases when knitting the lace sections that feature in some of the designs.

Increases

The designs feature three ways of increasing stitches: m1 (make 1); inc1 (increase 1; and yrn (yarn round needle; also called a yarnover).

M1

1

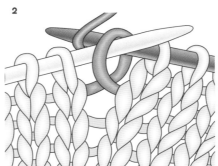

2

Inc1

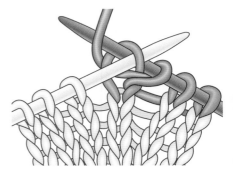

With your right-hand needle, pick up the loop lying between the stitch just worked and the next stitch (1). Knit into the back of the loop (2) to make the extra stitch; knitting into the back twists the yarn and prevents a hole appearing in the fabric.

This increase is made by knitting into the back and front of one stitch. Knit into the front of the stitch, but do not slip it off the needle, then knit again into the back of the stitch, and slip the stitch off the left-hand needle.

Yrn

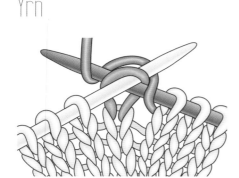

I use the abbreviation 'yrn' (yarn round needle). How you take the yarn round the needle depends on what stitch you are working – knit or purl. If you are on a knit stitch and then have to purl the next stitch, take the yarn to the front between the two needles and then take the yarn back over the right-hand needle and then again between the two needles. If the yrn is between two knit stitches, take the yarn between the two needles, then take the yarn back over the right-hand needle.

Decreases

The designs feature a number of ways of decreasing stitches: k2tog or p2 tog (knit or purl two stiches together); k2togtbl (knit two stitches together through the back loop) and s1 k1 psso (slip one, knit one, pass the slipped stitch over). To create a neat edging and an easier edge to pick up stitches or sew up, I do all my increases and decreases one or two stitches in from the edge of the row.

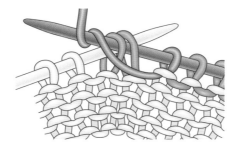

P2tog

The p2tog decrease is similar to k2tog except backwards! Purl into the first stitch, then purl into the second stitch at the same time (again treating them as if they were one stitch), purl the two together and slip them both off the left-hand needle.

P3tog

Work as p2tog, but purl three stitches instead of two.

K2tog

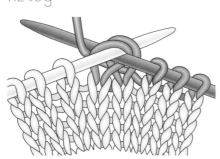

To work this decrease, knit into the second stitch on the left-hand needle and then the first one at the same time as if they were one, knit the two stiches together and slip them both off the left-hand needle.

K2togtbl

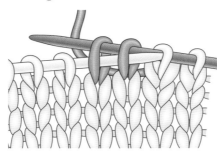

In some patterns, you can create a professional-looking finish if the decreases slant in the direction of the shaping, for example on a neck decrease. To do this, the k2tog is done through the back of the stitches or loops, hence the abbreviation 'k2togtbl' – knit two stitches together through the back loop.

Insert the right-hand needle into the back of the first stitch, then into the back of the second stitch on the left-hand needle, treating them as if they were one stitch, knit the two stitches together, and slip off needle.

S1 k1 psso

This method creates a decrease that slants in the same direction as k2togtbl. Slip the next stitch from the left-hand needle onto the right-hand needle (don't do anything to it, just slip it). Knit the next stitch on the left-hand needle as normal (1). On the right-hand needle, take the second stitch (which is your slipped stitch) over the first stitch and drop it off the needle (2).

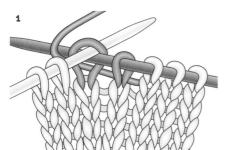

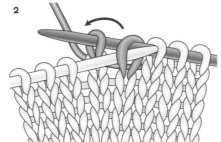

Cables and crossed stitches

Several of my designs feature cable and mock cable stitch patterns. These are used for different effects. In the Kimono-sleeved smock, for example, the cable pattern is worked all over in a fine gauge and creates a close fit to the upper portion of the sweater. In the *Cosy cables sweater,* a thicker-gauge cable pattern is worked in narrow vertical bands held between bands of reverse stockinette stitch.

Cables

The C4F (Cable four front) and C4B (Cable four back) cable stitch pattern is used in the *Cosy cables sweater, Huggable hoodie* and *Kimono-sleeved smock.* However, the cables are arranged in different ways on each design to create a different look and effect on the knitted garment.

C4F

1

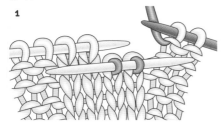

2

When cabling four stitches, you can use a cable needle if you want to. Sometimes I do, sometimes I don't, depending on the yarn. If the yarn is pure wool, or has a high wool content, I do not use a cable needle. If I'm working with a cotton yarn then I do. This is because cotton yarn doesn't have a lot of stretch.

If you use a cable needle, slip the next two stitches onto the cable needle and leave at the front of work (1), knit two stitches from the left-hand needle, then knit two stitches from the cable needle (2).

If you choose not to use a cable needle, miss the first two stitches on the left-hand needle, knit into the back of the third and fourth stitches, then knit into the front of the first stitch and then the second stitch, slipping all stitches off the left-hand needle.

C4B

1

2

I explain C4B as the opposite to C4F. If you use a cable needle, slip the next two stitches onto a cable needle and leave at the back of the work (1), knit two stitches from the left-hand needle, then knit two from the cable needle (2).

If you choose not to use a cable needle, miss the first two stitches on the left-hand needle, knit into the front of the third and then fourth stitches, then knit into the back of the first stitch and then the second stitch, slipping all stitches off the left-hand needle.

Crossed stitches

Crossed or twisted stitches are a way of creating a cable look, or mock cable, without having to use a cable needle. Usually mock cables involve twisting single stitches over each other (whereas 'full' cables usually involve twisting at least two stitches). I have used a mock cable pattern on the Shawl-collar cardigan.

Honeycomb cable

C2B

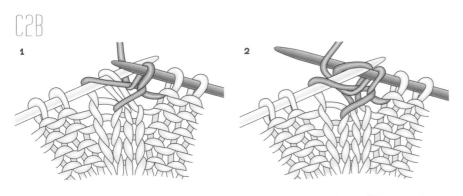

For C2B, miss the first stitch on the left-hand needle and knit into the front of the second stitch (1). Do not slip the worked stitch off the needle, but knit into the front of the first stitch (the 'missed stitch') (2). Slip both the stitches off the needle together.

Mock cable

C2F

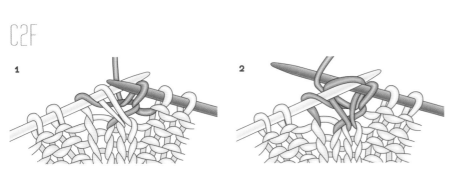

For C2F, knit the second stitch on the left-hand needle through the back, working behind the first stitch (1). Then knit into the front of the first stitch (2). Slip both the stitches off the needle together.

Cable bands

Knitting with beads

Knitting with beads is a lovely way to embellish a knitted garment, adding extra glamour and sparkle. *The Ruffled up vest top* features knitted-in beads to form a border around the V-neck. The button loop is also beaded.

Threading the beads

For this design, the beads need to be threaded onto the yarn before you start.

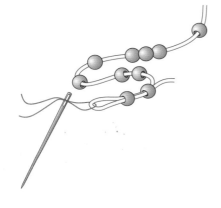

Before you pick up the stitches for the neck, thread your beads onto the yarn. Sometimes you can obtain beads large enough to thread directly onto the yarn. However, I used a mohair yarn and very small beads, which means I had to use a very fine sewing needle to thread the beads to the yarn, as you need the needle to pass through the hole in the beads easily.

A trick I use is to get some sewing cotton, tie a knot in the ends, and thread the yarn through the sewing-cotton loop. Thread the beads onto the yarn by putting them onto the needle and then pulling them down the sewing cotton and yarn.

Thread on all the beads suggested.

Binding off with beads

One bead is added to each stitch as you bind off the edging around the neckline.

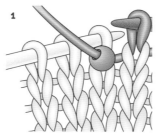 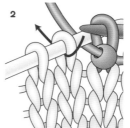

To position the bead into place on the bound-off edge, knit the first stitch then bring the yarn to the front of the work by taking the yarn between the two needles. Push a bead into place so it is sitting over the stitch on the left-hand needle (1), slip this stitch, take the yarn back and slip the stitch back onto the left-hand needle (2), knit and then bind off as normal by taking the second stitch on the right-hand needle over the first stitch.

The beaded loop

On the Ruffled up vest top, I have added a beaded loop to secure the button. This is very easy to make. The number of beads you need depends on how big your button is; I used 15. Thread the beads onto the yarn. Secure the ends together with a knot, thus making a loop. Then secure the ends into place opposite the button. I did this by knotting them into the bound-off edge and threading the ends in.

Buttonbands and buttonholes

Quite a few of the designs in this book feature buttons. Some of these are decorative features, such as the buttons on the shoulders of the *Push the boat out sweater*, and the buttons on the straps of the *On the button tank top* (although these buttons can be undone if necessary). The others are functional buttons that hold the garment closed.

There are two basic ways to knit a buttonband; either the buttonband is knitted in with the main parts of the garment (and therefore is included in the instructions for the left front and right front), or the buttonband is made by picking up stitches (see page 122) along the front edges of the item.

Knitted-in buttonbands

The *Great lengths coat* features a knitted-in buttonband. In this case, the buttonband is worked in garter stitch, so it creates a distinct border from the ribbed section at the top of the garment and the stockinette section of the lower part.

Picked-up buttonbands

The *Twice as nice cardigans*, *Shawl-collar cardigans* and *Huggable Hoodie* all feature picked-up buttonbands. The *hoodie* and the *Shawl-collar cardigans* feature ribbed buttonbands, whereas the *Twice as nice cardigan* buttonbands are worked in garter stitch. Picked-up buttonbands run vertically down the garment. In the case of the *Shawl-collar cardigan* and the *hoodie*, this becomes a design feature, as the buttonband is expanded and turned into the fold-down collar or the hood. In the *Twice as nice cardigans*, the garter-stitch edge creates a neat frame to the ribbed pattern of the rest of the garment.

Buttonholes

The same technique is used to create buttonholes whether on a knitted-in or picked-up buttonband; you simply create an eyelet by working a yarnover followed by a decrease (usually k2tog; see page 117). A single yarnover usually leaves a big enough hole to accommodate the button, especially as knitted fabric is stretchy and yielding.

Buttons

A button might seem like an insignificant accessory, but to me the button is like the icing on the cake; it completes the garment. I always choose my buttons when I have finished the garment. I take my garment to the button shop and place the buttons onto the garment to see which buttons work best. I find this is the best way to choose, especially because the texture and colour of the yarn can look different when knitted to when it is in a ball. It also means you can buy the right-sized button and the one that best complements the yarn.

Picking up stitches

Picking up stitches is a way of turning bound-off or edge stitches into live stitches so you can knit an extra piece onto a garment. You can pick up stitches on either the horizontal or vertical edges of a knitted piece.

Picking up stitches on a horizontal edge

In my patterns I like everything to be simple and as easy as possible. So when it comes to picking up stitches on a horizontal edge, I always leave these stitches on a holder and do not bind them off. This means that you can knit the stitches in one easy go, without having to pick up stitches, which can take a little longer.

Picking up stitches on a vertical edge

As I said in the section on buttonbands (page 121), there are a number of designs where you will pick up stitches on a vertical edge in order to form a buttonband. This technique can be a little tricky as you need to calculate how many stitches you pick up, and this is not as clear as with a horizontal edge where you can see the tops of the bound-off stitches. You can divide the edge up with evenly spaced safety pins or loops of spare thread if that helps (1).

I always work my increases and decreases one or two stitches in from the edge of a row to create a neat edge for picking up stitches. I never do this on the edge stitch as it can create an uneven finish or unnecessary holes.

In my patterns I ask you to pick up stitches on the right sides. With the right side facing, insert your needle into the hole between the edge 'v' stitch and the next one, take the yarn around the needle as if you were doing a knit stitch, and pull the loop through the fabric (2). Repeat the process again until all the stitches are picked up.

1

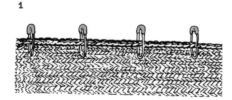

2

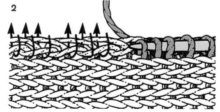

Finishing

There are a few knitting tips that you will need to know to achieve a really professional-looking finish to your garment. It's worth paying attention to details such as how you join in new balls of yarn, picking up dropped stitches, and weaving in your yarn ends at the end of the project.

Joining new balls of yarn

You can get through quite a few balls of yarn when making a garment, so it's worthwhile to make a neat job of joining in the new ball. It is best to join the yarn on the seam edge rather than in a middle of a row. This is because a new ball joined in the middle of a row can sometimes unravel and create a hole, or, in most instances when threading the ends into the fabric it can create an ugly twist in the stitches.

Dropped stitches

Everyone has dropped more than one stitch in their knitting history, and there can be many reasons for this. Depending on where the stitch is dropped or whether it is a knit or purl stitch depends on how you pick it up.

I reluctantly suggest that if the stitch is more than a row away you should unravel or unknit the knitting to the dropped stitch. I suggest this because I have picked up many stitches that are many rows away and I am never happy with the end result. It is okay, but not perfect! It might seem like an annoyance when it happens but it will be worth it.

If the dropped stitch is just in the row below then this is relatively easy to pick up. For a knit stitch, undo back to where the stitch is dropped, insert the right-hand needle into the front of the dropped stitch, making sure the strand is behind the stitch. Put the stitch back onto the left-hand needle. Put the right-hand needle through the centre of the stitch, catch the strand and pull through the stitch. When the strand is secure on the right-hand needle, slip off the stitch on the left-hand needle.

Weaving in ends

Where possible I weave in all ends along the edges after sewing up. This creates a neat edging and you cannot see the ends as they are hidden in the edges. If you weave in ends in the middle of the front or back it can be very obvious, even if you try to be as careful and neat as possible.

Joining pieces

All my designs are knitted in pieces, like the pattern pieces you would find in a sewing pattern. How you join the pieces will have a significant impact on how well the garment turns out. You don't want lumpy, bumpy seams or sleeves that bunch up awkwardly round the shoulders. Take care over the finishing of your garment and look fabulous when you wear it!

The order of making up

For the three sleeveless items, you will first join the shoulder seams, then sew the side seams.

For all the other items, you will first join the shoulder seams, then sew the sleeve head into the shoulder, then join the sleeve seams and the side seams.

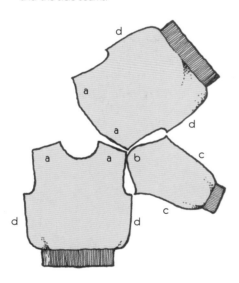

a Shoulder seams
b Sleeve head
c Sleeve seams
d Side seams

Joining the shoulder seams

Sewing the seams together

When you join the shoulder seams you will be joining two bound-off edges together.

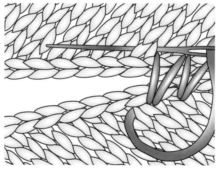

Lay the two seams together, right sides facing. Attach the yarn at one end. Insert the sewing needle threaded with yarn under the next stitch adjacent to the binding-off on one shoulder, then under the corresponding stitch on the second shoulder. Repeat to the end of the seam.

Three-needle bind-off

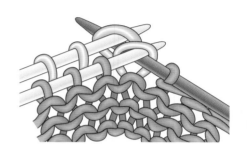

Another technique that I use is the three-needle bind-off. This involves ignoring an instruction in the pattern. Instead of binding off the stitches for the shoulders, leave these on a holder. When you have completed the back and front (or fronts), the pattern will then instruct you to join the shoulder seams.

You will need three knitting needles for this technique: the two that you used to knit the piece, and a third needle the same size. Take the stitches for the back piece off the holder and put them on a needle. Repeat this for the front, putting the stitches on the second needle. With the right sides together, hold the two needles together in your left hand, facing the same direction, as if both needles were one. Take the third knitting needle in your right hand and start to bind off, treating the two needles in your left hand as if they were one. This means you insert your needle into the first stitch on the first needle and into the first stitch on the second needle, then knit both of the stitches. Do this with the second stitch, and then slip the first stitch on the right-hand needle over the second stitch. Repeat this until all the stitches have been bound off.

Sewing in a sleeve

When you sew in the sleeve, you have to first line up the top of the sleeve head so that the middle point of it exactly aligns to the join of the shoulder seam. It helps to put some safety pins or tailor tacks in to keep everything in place while you sew the seam.

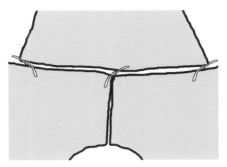

When I join a sleeve to an armhole, I find the middle of the sleeve head by folding it in half and marking the centre with a pin. I then place this pin to the shoulder seam and secure it into place with another pin. I then pin the edges of the sleeve head to the edge of the armhole, so that I can ease the rest of the sleeve edge into place. I then sew the sleeve head into place with mattress stitch, which is worked with the right side of the garment facing you.

Sewing the sleeve and side seams

There are several ways of sewing up the side seams: back stitch, slip stitch or mattress stitch. You can use the same techniques for sewing up sleeve seams and body seams. You need to work with the wrong side out for both the back stitch and slip stitch types of seams, while mattress stitch is worked with the right side facing out. I prefer mattress stitch. This is a basic technique that changes slightly depending on the stitches used.

Joining stockinette stitch side seams

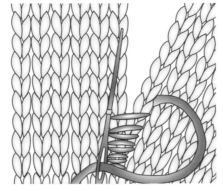

To me mattress stitch is a magical stitch that makes sewing up enjoyable – especially because you can use a different coloured thread if you want to and it will not show on the right side!

With the right sides facing, work one stitch in from the edge. When looking at stockinette stitch, there are visible 'V's. In between these 'V's, when the knitting is slightly pulled apart, there are bars. These are the bars that are used in mattress stitch; the needle is woven in and out of them. Starting at one side, and using a darning needle, insert the needle under the first two bars and up, then insert the needle at the same point on the other side, going under and behind the first two bars. Go to the other side, inserting the needle into the same place where the thread came. After you have completed this for a few centimetres/inches, pull the yarn and watch the two sides come together with an invisible seam! Remember to weave backwards and forwards between the two sides, and do not sew into the sides at all.

This is a technique that can also be used for joining ribbed edges.

Joining garter stitch side seams

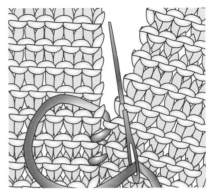

Joining garter stitch side seams uses the same technique at the mattress stitch explained above, except this time it uses the little bumps of the garter stitch, and instead of going back into the stitch just sewn you zigzag across, weaving into the next stitch.

Aftercare

Once you have put a lot of time, energy and effort into knitting a beautiful garment, that garment deserves to be cherished and looked after for the whole of its wearable life. Take some care over the washing and storing of your handknits and they will form the heart of your wardrobe for years to come.

Washing

To make sure your handknits last for years and years, I always recommend handwashing. All garments, regardless of yarn thickness or fibre content, should be treated as if they were delicate fibres. All balls of yarn carry labels with instructions on how to care for the yarns; some manufacturers even recommend dry-cleaning only. In these instances, do a test on a sample of the yarn before handwashing the finished garment.

Natural fibres will almost certainly shrink when washed in a machine, even at low temperatures. The very nature of the drum on a washing machine can create excess rubbing and this creates extra wear and tear on the delicate fabrics.

Where possible, buy a detergent specifically recommended for wool or delicate fabrics. For optimum results, turn the garment inside out and gently handwash in lukewarm water, rinsing thoroughly. To remove excess water after washing, roll the garment inside a large towel. Some knitters place the garment inside a pillowcase and put it into the washing machine on a gentle wool spin cycle.

Dry your garment flat, out of direct sunlight and gently pull it back into shape while damp. Never put the handknit into a tumble dryer!

Pressing should be done gently with a steam iron (or on the wool setting over a damp cloth). Again, gently pull the garment back into shape and do not press too much.

Storing

Always store your handknits flat. Do not hang them up, as this can pull them out of shape. Some knitters use mothballs or store their garments in plastic bags. I find that lavender is a good alternative to help deter insects.

International suppliers

Below are listed all the distributors, manufacturers and retailers whose yarns were featured in this book. The distributors will be able to recommend a good local yarn shop or internet shop, while the manufacturers and retailers may offer a mail-order or online retail service.

Colinette
UK: Colinette Yarns
Units 2-5
Banwy Workshops
Llanfair Caereinion
Powys, SY21 0SG
Tel: 01938 810128
www.colinette.com

USA: Unique Kolors Ltd
28 N. Bacton Hill Road
Malvern, PA, 19355
www.uniquekolors.com

Habu
UK: K1 Yarns
136 Queen Margaret Drive
Glasgow, G20 8NY
Tel: 0141 5760113

K1 Yarns
89 West Bow
Edinburgh, EH1 2JP
Tel: 0131 2267472
www.k1yarns.com

USA: Habu Textiles
135 West 29th Street
Suite 804
New York, NY, 10001
Tel: 212 239 3546
www.habutextiles.com

Katia
Canada: Diamond Yarn Ltd
155 Martin Ross Avenue
Unit 3 Toronto
Ontario, M3J 2L9
Tel: 416 736 6111
www.diamondyarn.com

Spain: Av. Catalunya s/n
Aptdo 138 08296
Castellbell i el Vilar
Barcelona
Tel: 34 93 834 02 01
www.katia.es

USA: Knitting Fever Inc
315 Bayview Ave
Amityville
New York, NY, 11701
Tel: 516 546 3600
www.knittingfever.com

Malabrigo
Canada: Diamond Yarn Ltd
155 Martin Ross Avenue
Unit 3 Toronto
Ontario, M3J 2L9
Tel: 416 736 6111
www.diamondyarn.com

UK: First 4 Yarns
23 Station Road
Knighton
Powys, LD7 1DT
Tel: 01547 529111
www.first4yarns.com

USA: Malabrigo Yarn
8424 NW 56th St 80496
Miami FL 33166
www.malabrigoyarn.com
Tel: 786 866 6187

Uruguay: Malabrigo Yarn
Gaboto 1277
Montevideo 11200

Debbie Bliss, Louisa Harding and Mirasol
Canada: Diamond Yarn Ltd
155 Martin Ross Avenue
Unit 3 Toronto
Ontario, M3J 2L9
Tel: 416 736 6111
www.diamondyarn.com

Germany: Designer Yarns
(Deutschland) GmbH
Sachsstrasse 30
D-50259 Pulheim Brauweiler
Tel: 49 2234 205453
www.designeryarns.de

UK and Europe: Designer Yarns Ltd
Units 8-10
Newbridge Industrial Estate
Pitt Street
Keighley, BD21 4PQ
Tel: 01535 664222
www.designeryarns.uk.com

USA: Knitting Fever Inc
315 Bayview Ave
Amityville
New York, NY, 11701
Tel: 516 546 3600
www.knittingfever.com

Noro
Australia/New Zealand:
Prestige Yarns Pty Ltd
PO Box 39
Bulli, NSW 2516
Tel: 61 (0) 2 4285 6669
www.prestigeyarns.com

Belgium and Holland: Pavan
Meerlaanstraat 73
9860 Balegem (Oosterzele)
Tel: 32 9221 8594
pavan@pandora.be

Canada: Diamond Yarn Ltd
155 Martin Ross Avenue
Unit 3 Toronto
Ontario, M3J 2L9
Tel: 416 736 6111
www.diamondyarn.com

Denmark: Fancy Knit
Hovedvejen 71
8586, Oerum Djurs Ramten
Tel: 45 5946 2189
Email: roenneburg@mail.dk

Finland: Duo Design
Kaikukuja 1 c 31
00530, Helsinki
Tel: 358 (0) 9 753 1716
www.duodesign.fi

France: Elle Tricote
8 Rue Du Coq (La Petite France)
67000 Strasbourg
Tel: 33 8823 0313
www.elletricote.com

Germany, Austria, Switzerland
and Luxembourg: Designer Yarns
(Deutschland) GmbH
Sachsstrasse 30
D-50259 Pulheim Brauweiler
Tel: 49 2234 205453
www.designeryarns.de

Italy: Emmepieffe Srl
Via dei Ronchi 45/1
10091 Alpignano, Torino
Tel: 39 (0) 11 966 2655
emmepieffesrl@virgilio.it

Japan: Eisaku Noro & Co Ltd
55 Shimoda Ohibino Azaichou
Ichinomiya Aichi, 491 0105
Tel: 81 586 51 3113
www.eisakunoro.com

Spain: Oyambre Needlework SL
Balmes
200 At. 4
08009, Barcelona
Tel: 34 (0) 93 487 2672
info@oyambreonline.com

Sweden: Hamilton Design
Storgatan 14
64730, Mariefred
Tel: 46 (0)159 12006
www.hamiltondesign.biz

UK: Designer Yarns Ltd
Units 8-10
Newbridge Industrial Estate
Pitt Street, Keighley
West Yorkshire
BD21 4PQ
Tel: 01535 664222
www.designeryarns.uk.com

USA: Knitting Fever Inc
315 Bayview Ave
Amityville
New York, NY, 11701
Tel: 516 546 3600
www.knittingfever.com

Index